THOMSON
PREPARATION
COURSE FOR THE
TOEIC® TEST

1

Thomson Asia Pte Ltd

Singapore • Albany • Belmont • Bonn • Cincinnati • Detroit • Johannesburg
London • Madrid • Melbourne • Mexico City • New York • Paris • Tokyo • Toronto

First published 1998
International Thomson Asia ELT
60 Albert Street
#15-01 Albert Complex
Singapore 189969

The publication of **Thomson Preparation Course for the TOEIC® Test 1** was directed by the International Thomson Asia ELT Team:

- Karen Chiang, *ELT Director*
- Christopher Wenger, *Senior Development Editor*
- Joan Quick, *Development Editor*
- Teri Tan, *Production Editor*
- Connie Wai, *Production Co-ordinator*
- Agnes Malinis, *Copy Editor*

- Additional editorial support provided by Jody Stern

Cover design by Raketshop Design Studio, Philippines

Printed by Chong Moh Offset Printing Pte Ltd, Singapore

1 2 3 4 5   02 01 00 99 98
ISBN 0-534-83521-X

CONTENTS

Author's Acknowledgements

I'd like to thank several people who helped conceptualize and actualize *Thomson Preparation Course for the TOEIC® Test 1*. First, thanks to Karen Chiang whose idea they were. Second, many thanks to my editor Chris Wenger who also served as photoscourer and project optimist. Third, I'm deeply indebted to my copy editor extraordinaire, Jody Stern. Finally, thanks to my husband, Avishai Shafrir, who patiently helped with math problems, suggested topics, and role-played dialogues, as well as to Patty Brickett, who enthusiastically brainstormed "office conversations" while sitting through swim meets. These books are lovingly dedicated to my parents Melvyn and Jeannette Ostroff Steinberg.

To the Test-taker...

The goal of the *Thomson Preparation Course for the TOEIC® Test* is to familiarize you with the format, directions, difficulty level, and substance of actual TOEIC® tests. After taking the three sample tests and reviewing the answers and explanations, you should know what is to be expected on the TOEIC® test. The point is not for you to memorize any of the questions and answers on the sample tests, as none of these questions will appear in the actual test. Rather, these tests will indicate your general strengths in English as well as the weaknesses you need to overcome before taking an actual TOEIC® test. The value of this book can be measured by comparing the score of your first practice test with subsequent tests.

Test-taking Tips

Before taking a sample test...

1. Increase your general knowledge of English. The purpose of the TOEIC® test is to measure your general English ability. Improving your ability in English takes time and should include work in all four skills: listening, speaking, reading, and writing, as well as specific work in grammar and vocabulary.

2. Prepare yourself by carefully studying the directions for each part of the TOEIC® test. The directions are **always** the same on each test. Make sure you are familiar with the structure of each part and what is expected of you. This will allow you simply to glance at the directions when you take the test, saving you valuable time.

While taking a sample test...

1. Try to create as authentic a test-taking environment as possible by doing the following:
    *   time yourself strictly as instructed
    *   do an entire test in one sitting
    *   do not eat, drink, or leave the room
    Following these suggestions will help give you an idea of how to manage your time most effectively during the test.

2. **Always** guess. There is no penalty for a wrong answer on the TOEIC® test, so never leave an answer blank. If you run out of time, fill in one answer [either (A), (B), (C), or (D)] for every blank number on your answer sheet. There is no letter which is a better choice. Statistically you have a better chance of getting more answers correct if you choose the same letter.

After taking a sample test...

1. Correct your exam.

2. Carefully review the **Answers and Explanations** section. If there is a question or answer you still don't understand, ask a native English speaker or fluent colleague for clarification, or consult appropriate reference materials.

3. Analyze your strengths and weaknesses. If you had difficulty with Parts I–IV, try to find time every day to listen to English programs on the radio, or watch television programs or videos featuring native English speakers. If you had difficulty with Part V, focus on word forms. Be familiar with noun, verb, adjective, and adverb endings. If you had mistakes in Part VI, find a grammar text that can help you review the grammar items that were problematic. If you had difficulty with Part VII, read English newspapers and magazines that feature a variety of international and business-related readings and advertisements.

4. Do not take the next test immediately. If you carefully review the Answers and Explanations section and begin a program to improve your areas of weakness, you will see an improvement on your next test.

I hope these sample tests have been helpful and instructive. I look forward to developing additional materials for you. Good luck!

Roberta Steinberg

SCORE CONVERSION CHART

Raw Scores	Converted Scores: Listening	Converted Scores: Reading	Raw Scores	Converted Scores: Listening	Converted Scores: Reading
98-100	495	470	56	260	215
97	495	465	55	255	210
96	495	460	54	250	205
95	495	455	53	245	200
94	490	450	52	235	190
93	490	445	51	230	185
92	485	435	50	225	180
91	480	430	49	220	175
90	475	425	48	215	165
89	470	415	47	205	160
88	465	410	46	200	155
87	460	400	45	195	150
86	455	39	44	185	140
85	450	390	43	180	135
84	445	385	42	175	130
83	435	380	41	165	125
82	430	370	40	160	120
81	425	365	39	155	115
80	420	360	38	145	105
79	410	350	37	140	100
78	400	345	36	135	95
77	390	340	35	130	90
76	385	335	34	120	85
75	380	330	33	115	80
74	375	320	32	110	75
73	365	315	31	105	65
72	360	310	30	100	60
71	350	305	29	90	55
70	345	300	28	85	50
69	340	295	27	80	40
68	335	285	26	70	35
67	330	280	25	65	30
66	325	275	24	60	25
65	320	270	23	50	20
64	310	265	22	45	15
63	305	255	21	40	10
62	300	250	20	35	10
61	290	245	19	30	10
60	285	240	18	25	5
59	275	230	17	20	5
58	270	225	16	15	5
57	265	220	0-15	5	5

TEST

one

TEST OF ENGLISH FOR INTERNATIONAL COMMUNICATION

General Directions

This is a test of your ability to use the English language. The total time for the test is approximately two and a half hours. It is divided into seven parts. Each part of the test begins with a set of specific directions. Be sure you understand what you are to do before you begin to work on a part.

You will find that some of the questions are harder than others, but you should try to answer every one. There is no penalty for guessing. Do not be concerned if you cannot answer all of the questions.

Do not mark your answers in this test book. **You must put all of your answers on the separate answer sheet** that you have been given. When putting your answer to a question on your answer sheet, be sure to fill in the answer space corresponding to the letter of your choice. Fill in the space so that the letter inside the oval cannot be seen, as shown in the example below.

EXAMPLE

Mr. Palmer _____ with the president last month.
(A) meet
(B) meeting
(C) met
(D) to meet

Sample Answer: (A)   (B)   ●   (D)

The sentence should read, "Mr. Palmer met with the president last month."
Therefore, you should choose answer (C). Notice how this has been done in the example given.

Mark only **ONE** answer for each question. If you change your mind about an answer after you have marked it on your answer sheet, completely erase your old answer and then mark your new answer. You must mark the answer sheet carefully so that your score can be recorded accurately.

LISTENING COMPREHENSION

In this section of the test, you will have the chance to show how well you understand spoken English. There are four parts to this section, with special directions for each part.

Directions

For each question, you will see a picture in your test book and you will hear four short statements. The statements will be spoken just one time. They will not be written in your test book; therefore, you must listen carefully in order to understand what the speaker says.

When you hear the four statements, look at the picture in your test book and choose the statement that best describes what you see in the picture. Then, on your answer sheet, find the number of the question and mark your answer. Look at the sample picture.

EXAMPLE

Now listen to the four statements.

Example:
You will hear: (A)   The man is tearing the paper.
                  (B)   The man is signing his name.
                  (C)   The man is reading a letter.
                  (D)   The man is opening an envelope.

Statement (B), "The man is signing his name," best describes what you see in the picture. Therefore, you should choose answer (B).

GO ON TO THE NEXT PAGE

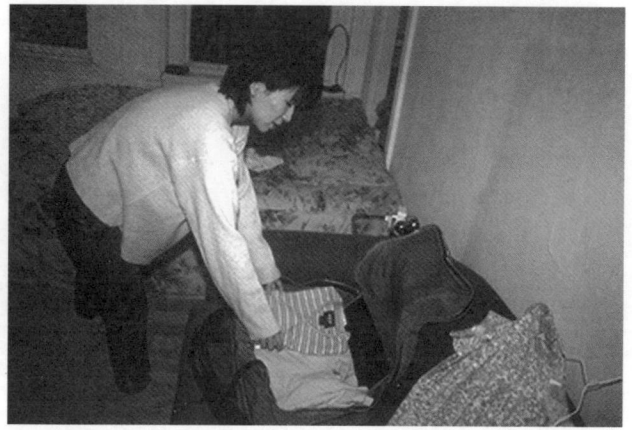

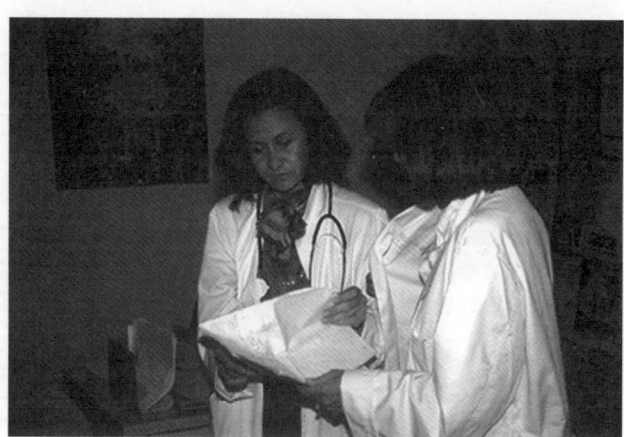

GO ON TO THE NEXT PAGE

10

11

12

13

14

15

GO ON TO THE NEXT PAGE ➤

16

17

18

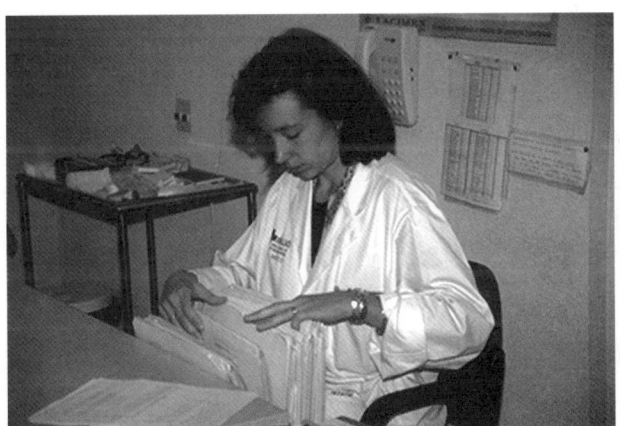

GO ON TO THE NEXT PAGE

Directions

In this part of the test, you will hear a question spoken in English, followed by three responses, also spoken in English. The question and the responses will be spoken just one time. They will not be written out for you; therefore, you must listen carefully to understand. You are to choose the best response to each question.

EXAMPLE

Now listen to a sample question.

You will hear: Good morning, John. How are you?

You will also hear: (A)   I am fine, thank you.
                     (B)   I am in the living room.
                     (C)   My name is John.

The best response to the question "How are you?" is choice (A), "I am fine, thank you." Therefore, you should choose answer (A).

21. Mark your answer on your answer sheet.

22. Mark your answer on your answer sheet.

23. Mark your answer on your answer sheet.

24. Mark your answer on your answer sheet.

25. Mark your answer on your answer sheet.

26. Mark your answer on your answer sheet.

27. Mark your answer on your answer sheet.

28. Mark your answer on your answer sheet.

29. Mark your answer on your answer sheet.

30. Mark your answer on your answer sheet.

31. Mark your answer on your answer sheet.

32. Mark your answer on your answer sheet.

33. Mark your answer on your answer sheet.

34. Mark your answer on your answer sheet.

35. Mark your answer on your answer sheet.

36. Mark your answer on your answer sheet.

37. Mark your answer on your answer sheet.

38. Mark your answer on your answer sheet.

39. Mark your answer on your answer sheet.

40. Mark your answer on your answer sheet.

41. Mark your answer on your answer sheet.

42. Mark your answer on your answer sheet.

43. Mark your answer on your answer sheet.

44. Mark your answer on your answer sheet.

45. Mark your answer on your answer sheet.

46. Mark your answer on your answer sheet.

47. Mark your answer on your answer sheet.

48. Mark your answer on your answer sheet.

49. Mark your answer on your answer sheet.

50. Mark your answer on your answer sheet.

Directions

In this part of the test, you will hear short conversations between two people. The conversations will not be written in your test book. You will hear the conversations only once; therefore, you must listen carefully.

In your test book, you will read a short question about each conversation. The question will be followed by four short answers. You are to choose the best answer to each question and mark it on your answer sheet.

51. What is said about the dinner?
    (A) It already began.
    (B) It will begin after the symposium ends.
    (C) Everyone must stay for it.
    (D) It will last half an hour.

52. How should the resume be delivered?
    (A) By fax
    (B) In person
    (C) By mail
    (D) By courier

53. What has been said about the receptionist?
    (A) That she is the best one so far.
    (B) That she is bad for the job.
    (C) That it is a good thing her two weeks are up.
    (D) That she does not like taking temporary jobs.

54. Why does the woman need a new computer?
    (A) For business applications
    (B) To increase memory space
    (C) To be able to use her CD-ROM
    (D) For word processing

55. Why is the man being transferred?
    (A) To help with budget negotiations
    (B) To be closer to home
    (C) To work somewhere else
    (D) To work at headquarters

56. Where is the report now?
    (A) In the mail
    (B) Waiting to be faxed
    (C) On Karen's desk
    (D) With Mr. Fisher

57. How is vacation time determined?
    (A) By seniority
    (B) Whoever asks first
    (C) According to family plans
    (D) By department heads

58. Why is Helmut upset?
    (A) He missed his plane.
    (B) He had a traffic accident.
    (C) He could not find a place to park.
    (D) He caused a traffic jam.

59. Where is the post office?
    (A) On Brattle Street
    (B) Four blocks away
    (C) Turn right from Brattle Street
    (D) In another town

60. What is wrong with the machine?
    (A) It needs toner.
    (B) It needs a maintenance check.
    (C) It cannot be fixed.
    (D) It is jammed.

GO ON TO THE NEXT PAGE

61. What is the man's problem?
- (A) He is not home during the day.
- (B) He does not live within the delivery radius.
- (C) He cannot decide which TV to buy.
- (D) He cannot afford the delivery charge.

62. When are vaccinations given?
- (A) Twice a year
- (B) Once a month
- (C) Every Thursday
- (D) Every two years

63. What needs to be located?
- (A) Fabric factories
- (B) The Philippine contact
- (C) The Korean order
- (D) Fabric dyes

64. What does the woman want to know?
- (A) Which bank the man uses
- (B) If the hotel exchanges money
- (C) Where the better exchange rate is
- (D) If he knows where the bank is

65. Who came up with the name change?
- (A) Management
- (B) The woman's team
- (C) The research firm
- (D) The man's group

66. How long will the man be in Brussels?
- (A) Until the plant is operational
- (B) Until the tenth of the month
- (C) Until the plant opens
- (D) Until he can get a flight out

67. What does the man want to do?
- (A) See how much was spent on advertising.
- (B) Pay off the company's debts.
- (C) Review this year's budget.
- (D) Advertise on TV.

68. What will he probably do?
- (A) Read a magazine on the plane.
- (B) Read the *New York Times*.
- (C) Go to the hotel bookstore.
- (D) Get another recommendation.

69. What is said about the banquet?
- (A) It will be in a different location than last year's.
- (B) It will be on board a ship.
- (C) It won't be as elegant as last year's.
- (D) It was difficult to book the Plaza Hotel.

70. Why isn't Pablo going to the concert?
- (A) It is raining.
- (B) He does not feel well.
- (C) It is too cold.
- (D) He has some things to check.

71. What does Tom want to do?
- (A) Wait fifteen minutes.
- (B) Go home first.
- (C) Make sure everything is OK in the office.
- (D) Phone home before going out.

72. What does the man learn?
- (A) He should have come before noon.
- (B) The *Tribune* is not sold there.
- (C) The *Tribune* is published in the morning.
- (D) There are no other English papers.

73. What does Shozo say?
- (A) He will let her know if he needs help.
- (B) He will be all set before the weekend.
- (C) He does not think he needs her.
- (D) He thinks he could use her help.

74. To whom is Kathy speaking?
   (A) Her mechanic
   (B) A colleague
   (C) Members of the task force
   (D) Someone at the gym

75. Why should they build something new?
   (A) To maintain the facade
   (B) To keep the location
   (C) To save time
   (D) To be economical

76. Where does this conversation take place?
   (A) Inside a building
   (B) Inside an elevator
   (C) At a library
   (D) At the inspector's office

77. How did the man decide which mortgage to take?
   (A) He chose the better deal.
   (B) The five-year variable had a lower rate.
   (C) He based the decision on his plan to move within five years.
   (D) The bank decided for him.

78. Who got bonuses?
   (A) All the supervisors
   (B) A lot of people
   (C) A limited number of supervisors
   (D) Those who didn't get pay raises

79. What are they discussing?
   (A) Restaurant locations
   (B) Where to get something to eat
   (C) Making coffee
   (D) What time they will finish the report

80. What is the man's problem?
   (A) He does not want to attend the meeting.
   (B) He cannot stay for the entire workshop.
   (C) He will not be in attendance.
   (D) He does not know when the workshop is.

GO ON TO THE NEXT PAGE

Directions

In this part of the test, you will hear several short talks. Each will be spoken just one time. They will not be written out for you; therefore, you will have to listen carefully in order to understand and remember what is said.

In your test book, you will read two or more questions about each short talk. The questions will be followed by four answers. You are to choose the best answer to each question and mark it on your answer sheet.

81. What day is it?
    (A) Thursday
    (B) Friday
    (C) Saturday
    (D) Sunday

82. What is the forecast for this morning?
    (A) A typhoon
    (B) Rain ending
    (C) Continued rain
    (D) Gentle winds

83. What does Grace Chin advise for today?
    (A) Not to drive
    (B) To leave coastal areas
    (C) To avoid rush hour
    (D) To take an umbrella

84. Where does the announcement take place?
    (A) In a department store
    (B) At the zoo
    (C) On a camping trip
    (D) At the seashore

85. Where is the child now?
    (A) With his parents
    (B) At police headquarters
    (C) On the mezzanine level
    (D) Shopping

86. What are the child's parents told to do?
    (A) Pay their bill.
    (B) Continue to look for him.
    (C) Call out the child's name.
    (D) Call the billing office.

87. Where does this introduction most likely occur?
    (A) On the waterfront
    (B) At a luncheon meeting
    (C) At Davio's Restaurant
    (D) In Mary Lilly's office

88. What does Mary Lilly do?
    (A) She's the personnel director.
    (B) She's in charge of publications.
    (C) She hires all new employees.
    (D) She supervises her colleagues.

89. When did she start working at the company?
    (A) Three years ago
    (B) Two years ago
    (C) A year ago
    (D) On Sunday

90. What does the corporation hope to do?
    (A) Relocate to Philadelphia.
    (B) Have its executives devise programs.
    (C) Encourage degree programs.
    (D) Improve executive performance.

91. What can be said about the courses?
    (A) They're brief.
    (B) They're only offered in Philadelphia.
    (C) They're prerequisites for the MBA.
    (D) They meet during the week.

92. Who will offer the courses?
    (A) Corporation executives
    (B) Specialist consultants
    (C) Tailors
    (D) Various employees

93. What kind of company is Golden Star?
    (A) An airline
    (B) A fruit distributor
    (C) A packaging company
    (D) An engineering firm

94. How are Golden Star's packages sent?
    (A) By trucks
    (B) In the first-class section
    (C) In cargo vessels
    (D) By air

95. How many distinct kinds of packaging were designed last year?
    (A) 1
    (B) 36,000
    (C) 44,000
    (D) Millions

96. What will change on December 1?
    (A) All popular music will become protected music.
    (B) A company will need permission to use popular music for advertising.
    (C) All popular music will become copyrighted.
    (D) All popular music will have an automatic license.

97. Which kind of music is expensive to use?
    (A) Protected music
    (B) Popular music
    (C) Music with an automatic license
    (D) Music without permission

98. What kind of products does Dogwood Technology make?
    (A) News communication systems
    (B) Telephones
    (C) Networked computers
    (D) Fax and voice message management systems

99. What percent did Dogwood shares fall?
    (A) Two
    (B) Eleven
    (C) Fifteen
    (D) Twenty-five

100. What did Bob Lynch blame the shortfall on?
    (A) Declining orders of voice message systems
    (B) Slow demand for fax equipment
    (C) The acquisition of Telecom Inc.
    (D) The development of interface cards

This is the end of the Listening Comprehension portion of the test. Turn to Part V in your test book.

GO ON TO THE NEXT PAGE

READING

In this section of the test, you will have the chance to show how well you understand written English. There are three parts to this section, with special directions for each part.

Directions

This part of the test has incomplete sentences. Four words or phrases, marked (A), (B), (C), (D), are given beneath each sentence. You are to choose the **ONE** word or phrase that best completes the sentence. Then, on your answer sheet, find the number of the question and mark your answer.

EXAMPLE

Because the equipment is very delicate, it must be handled with _____ .
(A) caring
(B) careful
(C) care
(D) carefully

The sentence should read, "Because the equipment is very delicate, it must be handled with care." Therefore, you should choose answer (C).

Now begin work on the questions.

101. The conference call is scheduled for 9:00, _____ Mr. Yamada may be out of the office.
(A) but
(B) either
(C) therefore
(D) which

102. All designers should use the new software to _____ spreadsheets.
(A) take
(B) give
(C) make
(D) cause

103. Unemployment is _____ to be lower this month.
(A) no
(B) may
(C) like
(D) apt

104. Rhode Island is the _____ state in the continental United States.
(A) small
(B) smallest
(C) smaller
(D) smallish

105. Ms. Ching's _____ was educated abroad.
- (A) college
- (B) collegial
- (C) collateral
- (D) colleague

106. Long-distance calls made after 5:00 can save _____ twenty percent.
- (A) over
- (B) under
- (C) at
- (D) beyond

107. Mr. Garcia will give your application his _____.
- (A) consistency
- (B) consolation
- (C) consideration
- (D) conservation

108. The decision must _____ immediately.
- (A) make
- (B) be made
- (C) made
- (D) to be made

109. We were surprised to learn there is an _____ demand for our products among teenagers.
- (A) increasing
- (B) increase
- (C) increases
- (D) increasingly

110. Everyone in the office was asked to _____ the gift for the retiring vice-president.
- (A) look after
- (B) give over
- (C) take up for
- (D) go in on

111. Direct deposit is a convenient way to reduce payroll time and _____.
- (A) money
- (B) salaries
- (C) paperwork
- (D) weight

112. Sources for start-up capital for new businesses _____ include personal savings.
- (A) seldom
- (B) ever
- (C) rare
- (D) unusually

113. The job _____ experience with several software programs.
- (A) equates
- (B) deletes
- (C) requires
- (D) resumes

114. The personnel director arranged for _____ to be paid weekly.
- (A) our
- (B) me
- (C) I
- (D) we

115. Mr. Lee relocated to the fifth floor while he _____.
- (A) had his office redecorated
- (B) his office redecorated had
- (C) his office had redecorated
- (D) had his redecorated office

116. Most nations have taken _____ to improve airport security.
- (A) levels
- (B) grades
- (C) steps
- (D) stairs

GO ON TO THE NEXT PAGE

117. _____ the summer, employees should attempt to stagger their vacation weeks.
(A) Behind
(B) Beside
(C) Across
(D) During

118. The marketing department was _____ the new product would be popular.
(A) concrete
(B) confident
(C) conscious
(D) continuous

119. Modular office furniture has become _____ popular due to its flexibility.
(A) widely
(B) width
(C) wide
(D) wide-open

120. Bids for the proposal must be received _____.
(A) prior to the deadline March first
(B) the March first deadline prior to
(C) to the March first deadline prior
(D) prior to the March first deadline

121. Gravity tends _____ an airplane on the ground.
(A) to keeping
(B) to be kept
(C) to keep
(D) keeping

122. The orientation begins at 8:00, with breakfast _____.
(A) simultaneous
(B) afterwards
(C) forward
(D) along

123. The e-mail on demand feature gives you free, unlimited access to _____ four hundred pages of additional information.
(A) beyond
(B) over
(C) less
(D) more

124. Department heads always make budgetary decisions _____.
(A) immediately
(B) timely
(C) yesterday
(D) shortly

125. Retiring Mr. Shah asked us all to please be sure to stay in _____ him.
(A) touched
(B) touch to
(C) touch with
(D) to touch

126. A "cash cow" is a business that has had strong sales, as well as _____ revenue.
(A) promissory
(B) incentive
(C) declining
(D) consistent

127. A letter of credit, _____ by a bank, guarantees a debt will be paid.
(A) provided
(B) adopted
(C) substituted
(D) predicted

128. Your coverage remains in _____ as long as you are a full-time employee.
(A) power
(B) effect
(C) supply
(D) respect

129. Computers function best when there is almost _____ heat or humidity.
(A) either
(B) no
(C) none
(D) neither

130. Company policy requires that letters of _____ be submitted in writing.
(A) recollection
(B) repercussion
(C) resignation
(D) recuperation

131. The company treasurer, to _____ you sent the forms, is on maternity leave.
(A) which
(B) her
(C) what
(D) whom

132. The directions state that the computer should be _____ while moving it.
(A) upright
(B) upheld
(C) uplift
(D) uptight

133. The use of brand-name products on film and television is _____ by lawyers.
(A) contorted
(B) lavished
(C) negotiated
(D) relented

134. _____ to inflation, deflation is a widespread decline in prices.
(A) Despite
(B) In contrast
(C) According
(D) Whereas

135. _____ faxes, e-mail permits the recipient to edit the message and work with the data sent.
(A) All alike
(B) Dislike
(C) Alike
(D) Unlike

136. Many companies have _____ direct marketing as a means of identifying customers.
(A) found
(B) hired
(C) understood
(D) adopted

137. Desktop video conferencing _____ around since the early 1990's.
(A) has been
(B) was
(C) had to be
(D) has been being

138. The types of franchised businesses _____ from auto dealerships to fast-food restaurants.
(A) move
(B) shift
(C) range
(D) encompass

139. Employees increasingly rely _____ end-of-the-year bonuses to supplement their incomes.
(A) to
(B) over
(C) on
(D) until

140. Improved technology is always a source of lower costs and a _____ to economic growth.
(A) tax
(B) spur
(C) gem
(D) digression

GO ON TO THE NEXT PAGE

Directions

In this part of the test, each sentence has four words or phrases underlined. The four underlined parts of the sentence are marked (A), (B), (C), (D). You are to identify the **ONE** underlined word or phrase that should be corrected or rewritten. Then, on your answer sheet, find the number of the question and mark your answer.

EXAMPLE

All <u>employee</u> are required <u>to wear</u> their <u>identification</u> badges <u>while</u> at work.
    A   B   C   D

Choice (A), the underlined word "employee," is not correct in this sentence. The sentence should read, "All employees are required to wear their identification badges while at work." Therefore, you should choose answer (A).

Now begin work on the questions.

141. A <u>three-year</u> study <u>has concluded</u> that
       A   B
frequent <u>shortest</u> vacations are
         C
<u>more beneficial</u> than infrequent longer ones.
       D

142. The <u>newest</u> computer has
      A
<u>totally and completely</u> captured <u>most of</u> the
         B   C
market share <u>throughout</u> the Northeast.
          D

143. Negotiators <u>for</u> the merger
         A
<u>they have decided</u> to postpone <u>subsequent</u>
      B   C
talks <u>until</u> the next fiscal year.
    D

144. The conference <u>has been postponed</u> <u>until</u>
                A   B
further notice <u>due to</u> a lack of adequate hotel
           C
<u>accommodation</u>.
    D

145. Visitors to Boston in the <u>near</u> future <u>will be</u>
                    A   B
<u>inconvenienced by</u> the downtown <u>highway's</u>
      C   D
construction.

146. In the 1970's there <u>have been</u> two
              A
<u>unsuccessful</u> attempts <u>to revive</u> the dollar
     B   C
coin <u>in the U.S.</u>
     D

147. Drawing is the act of making a design or
     A   B
image to use a line or tone on any suitable
       C   D
surface.

148. Joyce Chin, the treasurer and comptroller,
                  A
announced that she will be taking a new job
            B   C
as a consultant marketing.
         D

149. Congestion around the theater district is
          A
always more noticeable whenever there is a
         B   C
daytime matinee.
      D

150. Containerization is a method of shipping
               A
freight which help prevent damage
         B
by placing the cargo in large containers.
   C   D

151. A product or package should not be
        A
marketing as recyclable unless it can
    B   C
be collected.
    D

152. The Bank of New York, found in 1784, is
             A B
the sixth oldest company in the United
      C   D
States.

153. The upcoming telecommunications
      A
conference is expected to attract over
        B   C
50,000 people from through the world.
             D

154. The export manager is responsible for
             A
checking the bill of lading before they are
   B   C   D
mailed from the office.

155. The tiny nation has taken inflation and
          A
interest rates to record lows and cuts the
         B   C
government deficit.
    D

156. People can either create and purchase
    A   B
software containing programs that a
       C   D
computer uses to perform a task.

157. The effect of natural light, fresh air, smell,
     A   B
and color in the office is being studied by
             C
psychologists and architecture.
          D

158. The museum can be rent for evening
        A
corporate meetings, as well as for
   B   C   D
receptions.

159. Ms. Romero was asked to make a poll
            A
among the office workers as to their
   B   C
availability for working overtime.
     D

160. Although several outstanding candidates
           A
have submitted their resumes, there is no
     B   C
interviews scheduled at this time.
          D

GO ON TO THE NEXT PAGE ▶

Directions

The questions in this part of the test are based on a variety of reading material, such as notices, letters, newspaper and magazine articles, and advertisements. You are to choose the **ONE** best answer, (A), (B), (C), or (D), to each question. Then, on your answer sheet, find the number of the question and mark your answer. Answer all questions following a passage on the basis of what is **stated** or **implied** in that passage.

EXAMPLE

Read the following example.

> The Museum of Technology is designed for people to experience science at work. Visitors are encouraged to use, test, and handle the objects on display. Special demonstrations are scheduled for the first and second Wednesdays of each month at 1:30 p.m. Open Tuesday–Friday, 2:30–4:30 p.m., Saturday 11:00 a.m. –4:30 p.m., and Sunday 1:00–4:30 p.m.

When during the month can visitors see special demonstrations?
(A)   Every weekend
(B)   The first two Wednesdays
(C)   One afternoon a week
(D)   Every other Wednesday

The passage says that the demonstrations are scheduled on the first and second Wednesdays of the month. Therefore, you should choose answer (B).

Now begin work on the questions.

The International Mall on King George Street will open
its ten floors for business this Sunday, promising to be
this country's most luxurious shopping center.
Make sure you sample one of the arcade's twenty restaurants,
plan to see a film at one of the eight theaters, and
shop at over one hundred boutiques and department stores.

161. What is the International Mall?
  (A) A business headquarters
  (B) A hotel
  (C) A shopping center
  (D) A casino

162. How many stories are there in the Mall?
  (A) 8
  (B) 10
  (C) 20
  (D) 100

GO ON TO THE NEXT PAGE

Questions 163–165 refer to the following advertisement.

**Understanding the Workplace
Means Viewing It From All Perspectives**

World Workplace Symposium ● Toronto, Canada ● October 5-7

Only ONE event allows you to explore all aspects of a productive workplace.
World Workplace is where the professionals meet to learn and discuss
the latest ideas involved with providing an effective work environment.
Choose from 86 educational sessions and 22 round tables covering
a panorama of concepts pertaining to architecture, construction management,
design engineering, facility management, and real estate.
World Workplace activities provide you with relaxed, fun occasions to network
with workplace professionals from around the world.
These tremendous opportunities to make new connections will help you
communicate better and work more effectively to the benefit of
your company and your career.

163. What is World Workplace?
(A) A job fair
(B) A vacation resort
(C) An exposition
(D) An office complex

164. Why would someone attend World
Workplace?
(A) To investigate pollution control methods.
(B) To discover new career possibilities.
(C) To become a licensed real estate agent.
(D) To get ideas about effective work
environments.

165. Which field is NOT listed as one of the
sessions?
(A) Interior design
(B) Architecture
(C) Real estate
(D) Engineering

Amazing changes are sweeping Asia. Coincidentally, so are more of our nonstop flights from Minneapolis/St. Paul and Detroit.

Don't blink. Asia is changing so rapidly you might miss something. Fortunately, our new nonstop flights from Minneapolis/St. Paul and Detroit, in addition to our convenient connections when traveling from the East Coast and Southeast, make it easier than ever for you to keep up with Asia's remarkable transformation. Connecting in St. Paul can save you up to four hours from the East Coast. And the new state-of-the-art customs facility in Detroit makes it possible for you to whisk along with impressive efficiency. So while you may not be able to predict the next trend in Asia, there's one thing you can be certain of. As opportunities in Asia grow, so will Transcoast's ways of getting you there.

166. What service does Transcoast provide?
(A) West Coast connections to Asia
(B) Nonstop flights from Detroit to Asia
(C) Nonstop flights from the East Coast to Asia
(D) Flights within Asia

167. What is the benefit of flying from the East Coast to Asia via St. Paul?
(A) Learning about Asian opportunities.
(B) Viewing the customs facility.
(C) Saving time.
(D) Being able to fly nonstop from the East Coast.

GO ON TO THE NEXT PAGE

Questions 168–170 refer to the following notice.

IMPORTANT INFORMATION FOR RESERVE CREDIT CUSTOMERS

1 You may make payments by cash, check, or money order, by executing an appropriate transfer form, or by authorizing us to deduct the minimum payment due automatically from your checking account. To pay by mail, you must send us a transfer form allowing us to transfer funds from your checking or NOW account. If we receive the transfer form by 3:00 p.m. on any business day, the payment will be credited on that day.

2 If you think your bill is wrong, write us at the address printed on the front of your statement as soon as possible. We must hear from you no later than 60 days after we sent you the first bill on which the error or problem appeared. Please do not telephone us. Make sure you include your name, account number, and the amount of the suspected error. Please also explain what you think the error is. You do not have to pay any amount in question, but you are still obligated to pay the part of the bill not in question.

168. Which of these methods is NOT a way to make a payment?
(A) By cash
(B) By check
(C) By credit card
(D) By money order

169. What should you immediately do if you think the bill is wrong?
(A) Don't pay it.
(B) Write to them.
(C) Bring in the bill.
(D) Telephone them.

170. If you suspect an error, what must you pay?
(A) The amount in question
(B) All of the bill
(C) None of the bill
(D) The part not in question

ANNUAL TRUSTEES MEETING

The annual meeting of the Board of Trustees of Mount Ida College will be held at 10:00 a.m. on May 16th in the Faculty Dining Room prior to the commencement ceremony. Subjects to be discussed are tenure for six faculty members, the proposal to build a new gymnasium, plans for the college's Centennial in 2001, and adoption of three new degree programs: hotel management, physical therapy, and finance. If you need hotel arrangements, please call the personnel director at extension 2329 before May 1.

171. What is the main purpose of this announcement?
(A) To give the personnel director's extension.
(B) To inform members of a meeting.
(C) To invite trustees to commencement.
(D) To announce a change in the meeting.

172. What new program is being considered?
(A) Physical education
(B) The History of Mount Ida College
(C) Occupational therapy
(D) Finance

173. When will commencement be held?
(A) After the meeting
(B) Prior to the meeting
(C) At the college's centennial
(D) On May 1

GO ON TO THE NEXT PAGE

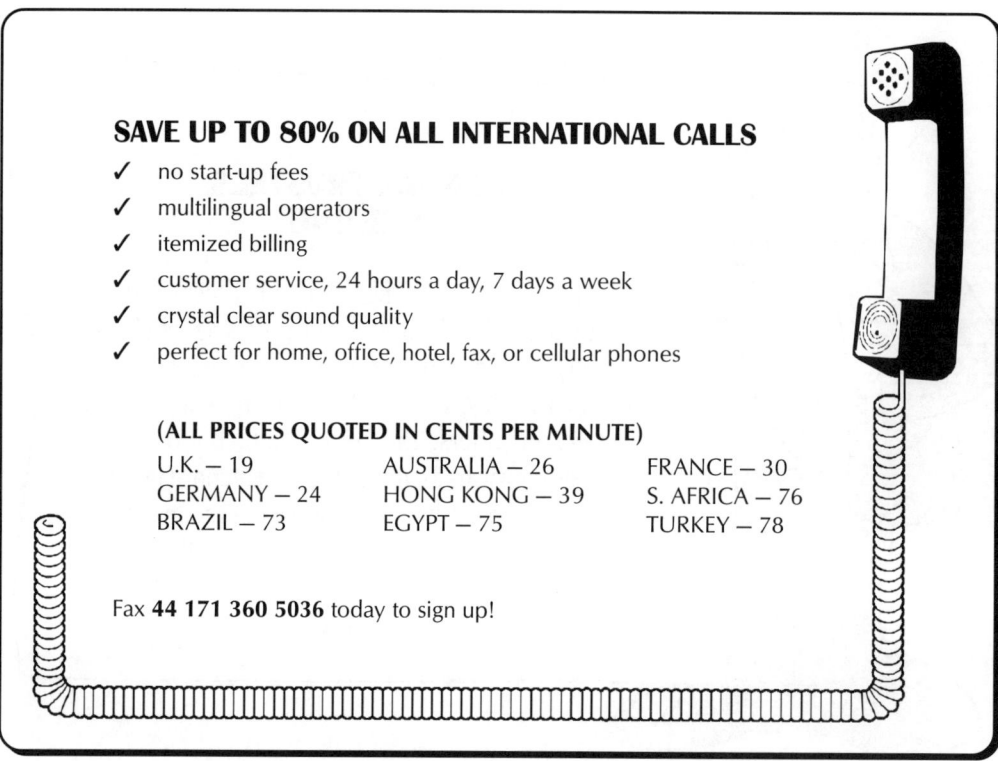

174. What does this company offer?
- (A) Interpreting services
- (B) Billing systems
- (C) Sound equipment
- (D) Phone service

175. How much would a ten-minute call to Egypt cost?
- (A) $7.30
- (B) $7.50
- (C) $7.80
- (D) $70.50

176. Why would someone want this service?
- (A) To receive a free cellular phone.
- (B) To be able to speak to operators in every country.
- (C) To receive information about each call.
- (D) To get the best international rates.

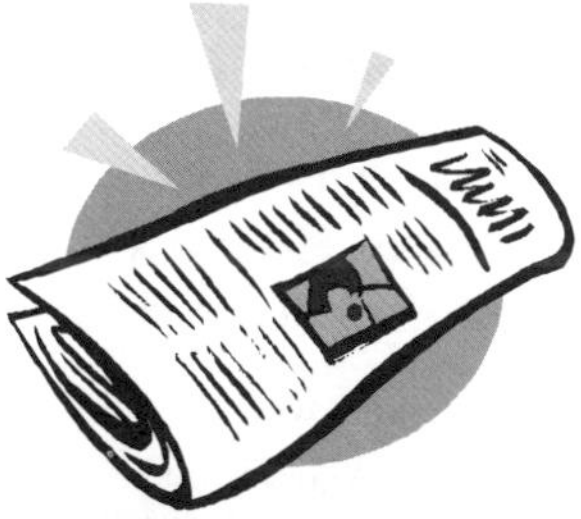

SUBSCRIBE TO Business Today
THE MAGAZINE FOR THE NEXT MILLENNIUM

ACT NOW and receive Business Today for only 79 cents an issue.

Cover price for 27 issues $79.65 ($2.95 an issue)

Your Cost $21.33 That's 73% off the $2.95 cover price!

You save $58.32

Just fill out this voucher:
Name: ___
Street: ___
City/State/Zip: ___

Check one:
☐ 24 months (106 issues) only 69 cents per copy.
☐ 12 months (53 issues) 79 cents per copy.
☐ 6 months (27 issues) 79 cents per copy

Please check:
☐ Payment enclosed
☐ Bill me later
☐ Renewal (attach label)

177. What can be said about the offer?
(A) At least four magazines arrive monthly.
(B) Twelve and twenty-four month subscriptions cost the same per copy.
(C) One must enclose a payment.
(D) Only new customers are eligible for the savings.

178. If this subscription is a renewal, what should the person do?
(A) Write down a credit card number.
(B) Attach the mailing label.
(C) Enclose a payment.
(D) Check to be billed later.

179. Which subscription length is the best value?
(A) Six months
(B) Twelve months
(C) Twenty-four months
(D) Twenty-seven months

GO ON TO THE NEXT PAGE

Questions 180–184 refer to the following advertisement.

WalkFit gives you twice the exercise of walking outdoors.

You know you need to exercise, but when? With a WalkFit, time isn't a problem. Minute for minute, WalkFit's total-body exercise is the efficient way to tone those jiggling muscles and feel wonderful.

Just 30 minutes, 4 times a week is all it takes, with the added convenience and safety of being in your own home. WalkFit helps you lose weight and gain energy fast! While you're enjoying the walking exercise you love, WalkFit is giving you a great upper-body workout, too. WalkFit's arm exerciser is the key, making it possible to target every major muscle group in your body simultaneously, for maximum total-body results in less time.

Ordinary walking machines, such as treadmills, simply can't exercise your whole body. In fact, just one hour on WalkFit burns an average of 850 calories. That's twice as many calories as motorized treadmills that work only your legs. Before you know it, you can drop inches and improve your cardiovascular fitness. Plus, you'll have more energy and less stress. Best of all, you'll be spending less time exercising!

Call for your free 30-day trial today.

180. What is WalkFit?
   (A) A fitness program
   (B) A workout manual
   (C) A leg exerciser
   (D) An exercise machine

181. What is NOT mentioned as an advantage of WalkFit over walking outdoors?
   (A) Cost
   (B) Convenience
   (C) Safety
   (D) Time

182. Approximately how many calories are burned in an hour of exercise on a motorized treadmill?
   (A) 212
   (B) 425
   (C) 1,275
   (D) 1,700

183. What is the recommended amount of time for maximum results?
   (A) 30 minutes every third day
   (B) 30 minutes a day
   (C) 120 minutes a day
   (D) 120 minutes a week

184. Why is WalkFit preferable to ordinary walking machines?
   (A) It is cheaper.
   (B) It works only the legs.
   (C) It focuses only on the upper body.
   (D) It exercises the entire body.

Questions 185–187 refer to the following advertisement.

Travel the world with Odyssey, the World's First Atlasphere.

This is not just a globe, but a three-dimensional computerized atlas of marvelous information. Touch any country with a special pointer, and Odyssey tells you the local time, the capital, the population, and other interesting facts. It even plays a native musical selection from the country you chose. The GeoZone cartridge contains geography games everyone will love. Plus, the Metropolis cartridge provides facts on over 500 cities. Updated information, including any changes anywhere in the globe, will be mailed to all purchasers annually.

185. How does Odyssey differ from traditional globes?
(A) It is two dimensional.
(B) It televises news from around the world.
(C) It is a computerized atlas.
(D) It rotates.

186. How does one select a country?
(A) With the GeoZone cartridge
(B) With a pointer
(C) By typing in the country name
(D) With the updated information

187. What is the function of the Metropolis cartridge?
(A) It tells you the local time.
(B) It contains games everyone will love.
(C) It provides facts on over five hundred cities.
(D) It plays native music selections.

GO ON TO THE NEXT PAGE

Questions 188–190 refer to the following announcement.

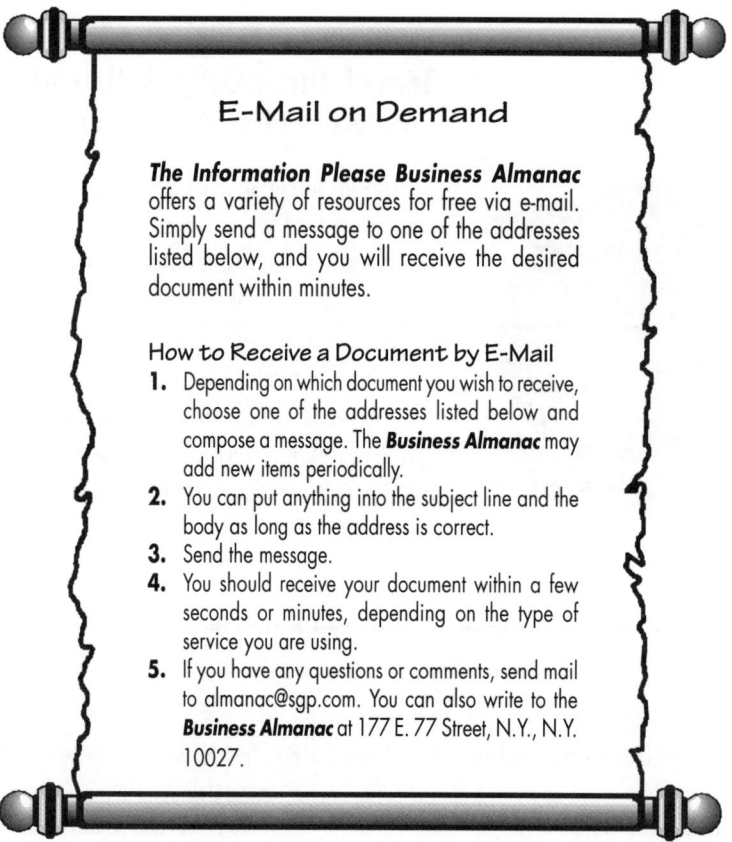

E-Mail on Demand

The Information Please Business Almanac offers a variety of resources for free via e-mail. Simply send a message to one of the addresses listed below, and you will receive the desired document within minutes.

How to Receive a Document by E-Mail

1. Depending on which document you wish to receive, choose one of the addresses listed below and compose a message. The **Business Almanac** may add new items periodically.
2. You can put anything into the subject line and the body as long as the address is correct.
3. Send the message.
4. You should receive your document within a few seconds or minutes, depending on the type of service you are using.
5. If you have any questions or comments, send mail to almanac@sgp.com. You can also write to the **Business Almanac** at 177 E. 77 Street, N.Y., N.Y. 10027.

188. What can be said about the documents offered?
(A) They are free.
(B) They are available to *Business Almanac* subscribers only.
(C) The number remains fixed.
(D) They can be obtained by writing away for them.

189. What determines the length of time an answer takes?
(A) Which document is requested
(B) The length of the message
(C) How far away the destination is
(D) The type of service you are using

190. What is listed after these five steps?
(A) E-mail instructions
(B) Addresses
(C) A questionnaire
(D) Additional steps

Questions 191–193 refer to the following advertisement.

Imagine Cruise Ships As Individual As The Destinations They Reach

Just off the beaten path, you'll discover a Europe that is delightfully unexpected. What better way to enjoy majestic ports of call along the Mediterranean than aboard the two most luxurious ships sailing these waters from early May through October.

Choose between the 350-guest *Empire Diamond* or the 180-guest *Song of Emeralds*. While both have been awarded six stars by *Brown's Guide to Worldwide Cruises*, each is individually remarkable. *Diamond's* innovative twin-hull design makes her the most stable ship on the seven seas. On the other hand, *Song of Emeralds'* smaller size brings you to destinations other ships cannot reach. While *Diamond* offers the highest space ratio of any ship in her class, *Song of Emeralds* features the highest crew-to-guest ratio in the industry. All of this means whichever ship you choose, you will have a wonderful experience seeing the best of Europe this year.

191. What do these ships have in common?
(A) Their size
(B) Their twin hulls
(C) Their crew-to-guest ratio
(D) Their six-star rating

192. When do these ships sail?
(A) Five months a year
(B) Six months a year
(C) Seven months a year
(D) Prior to May 1

193. Which of the following is NOT mentioned as a feature of *Song of Emeralds?*
(A) Its crew-to-guest ratio
(B) Its 180-guest capacity
(C) Its smaller size
(D) Its innovative twin hull

GO ON TO THE NEXT PAGE

Earn Your Business Degree: Commute to Class by Modem

Whether you're completing your bachelor's degree or preparing for graduate school, you can achieve your goal without ever leaving your keyboard. Our easy-to-use software will transport you to the University of Phoenix On-line Campus wherever you and your computer happen to be. Our instructors are seasoned by years of real-world business experience. All of our courses address issues you face every day.

Select from a distinguished array of degree programs in business, management, technology, and information systems — each designed specifically for adult professionals. Every course is dynamic, interactive, flexible, and loaded with the kind of material that you can put to use immediately. There's only one accredited university recognized for its experience and excellence in on-line programs. Visit the University of Phoenix Online Campus' web site today!

194. For whom is this program NOT designed?
(A) People completing a bachelor's degree
(B) Those ready for a graduate degree
(C) Adult professionals
(D) High school students with modem access

195. Which of the following is true about the program?
(A) Classes remain small even if many students register for a particular class.
(B) Students may live on campus if they desire.
(C) Instructors have years of practical experience.
(D) The program is currently seeking accreditation.

196. In order to participate in this program, what would one need?
(A) A ticket to Phoenix
(B) A fax machine
(C) A computer
(D) A videocassette recorder

To: All Department Heads
From: James Carlson, Vice-President
Date: March 7
Re: **Artificial Respiration Procedures**

It has come to our attention that employees need to be trained in administering artificial respiration in the case of an emergency. Please announce the posting of the following guidelines in a place readily accessible to everyone in your department.

Artificial respiration is mouth-to-mouth breathing, used in cases such as electric shock, drowning, or smoke inhalation. There is need for help when breathing movements stop, or lips, tongue, and fingernails become blue. When in doubt, apply artificial respiration until you get medical help. No harm can result from its use and delay may cost the patient his or her life. Start immediately. Seconds count.

For adults: Place patient on back with face up. Clear mouth and throat of any obstruction with your fingers.Lift the chin and tilt the head back. If air passage is still closed, pull chin up by placing fingers behind the angles of the lower jaw and pushing forward. Take a deep breath; place your mouth over patient's mouth, making a leak-proof seal. Pinch patient's nostrils. Blow into patient's mouth until you see the chest rise. Repeat twelve times a minute.

197. Who sent the memo?
(A) James Carlson
(B) Area doctors
(C) Department heads
(D) Employees

198. Why would one need to have artificial respiration administered?
(A) One wishes to swim for an extended period of time.
(B) One has breathed too much smoke.
(C) One's fever is too high.
(D) One is extremely fatigued.

199. How should obstacles in the throat be cleared?
(A) With the tongue
(B) By lifting the chin
(C) With one's fingers
(D) By pushing the jaw forward

200. What is NOT true about blowing into the patient's mouth?
(A) Stop once medical help arrives.
(B) Pinch the patient's nostrils first.
(C) Repeat twelve times a minute.
(D) Leave fingers in the patient's mouth to clear obstructions.

Stop! This is the end of the test. If you finish before time is called, you can go back to Parts V, VI, and VII and check your work.

Sample Item
M: (A) The man is tearing the paper.
    (B) The man is signing his name.
    (C) The man is reading a letter.
    (D) The man is opening an envelope.

1. *W:* (A) They are talking in the office.
    (B) The woman is holding some papers.
    (C) The man and woman are waiting in traffic.
    (D) They are crossing the street.

2. *M1:* (A) Both doors are closed.
    (B) A decoration is above each door.
    (C) People are exiting the elevator door.
    (D) One door is open.

3. *M2:* (A) The seamstress is sewing a coat.
    (B) The coat is already finished.
    (C) The seamstress is turning on the machine.
    (D) The seamstress is measuring the garment.

4. *W:* (A) The man is hanging up the phone.
    (B) The man is listening to someone on the phone.
    (C) The man is speaking into the receiver.
    (D) The phone has not been installed yet.

5. *M1:* (A) The woman is opening her bag for a customs check.
    (B) The suitcase is overweight.
    (C) The woman is packing for a trip.
    (D) The suitcase is already packed.

6. *M2:* (A) The doctor with the stethoscope is examining a patient.
    (B) The doctors are entering the waiting room.
    (C) The doctors are writing up a report.
    (D) The doctors are examining a file.

7. *W:* (A) There is no one available for help.
    (B) A woman is checking something on her monitor.
    (C) The women are in front of the desk.
    (D) Two employees are helping customers.

8. *M2:* (A) The tables are set.
    (B) The waiters are very busy.
    (C) Dinner is being served.
    (D) The restaurant is full.

9. *M1:* (A) Thousands of spectators are watching the parade.
    (B) Each man is holding a flag.
    (C) The men are wearing uniforms.
    (D) The men are marching in different directions.

10. *W:* (A) The boats are at the dock.
    (B) Several boats are in the water.
    (C) No one is rowing in the boats.
    (D) The water is very rough for the rowers.

11. *M2:* (A) There are different prices for the fruits and vegetables.
    (B) The vegetables are on the scale.
    (C) The fruits and vegetables are on the table.
    (D) The fruits and vegetables are being displayed outdoors.

12. *M1:* (A) There are cars on both sides of the building.
    (B) The building is ten stories high.
    (C) The construction is blocking the view of the building.
    (D) Many taller buildings surround the apartment house.

13. *W:* (A) Traffic is approaching in both directions.
    (B) The street is deserted.
    (C) Tall trees line both sides of the road.
    (D) There is one car on the four-lane highway.

14. *M1:* (A) The woman is waving to the man on the bicycle.
    (B) The woman is in front of the man.
    (C) The man and woman are riding on the same bicycle.
    (D) The man is waving to friends.

15. *M2:* (A) The women are looking in the shop window.
    (B) The women are washing the window.
    (C) The women are putting up a window display.
    (D) The women are installing a new window.

16. *W:* (A) The boy is throwing the ball.
    (B) The boy is kicking the ball.
    (C) The soccer ball is being caught.
    (D) The ball is on the ground.

17. *M2:* (A) An artist is painting at an outdoor market.
    (B) The paintings are at a museum.
    (C) The paintings are hanging on the wall.
    (D) People are shopping for paintings in the market.

18. *M1:* (A) The mother is pushing the baby.
    (B) The father is carrying the baby.
    (C) The parents are riding motorcycles.
    (D) The baby is in a stroller.

19. *W:* (A) The man has his arm around the woman's shoulder.
    (B) The woman is carrying the man across the street.
    (C) The man and woman are walking arm-in-arm.
    (D) The man is walking toward the woman in the parking lot.

20. *M2:* (A) The woman has set her folders out on her desk.
    (B) The woman is looking through her files.
    (C) The woman is making notes on one of her files.
    (D) The woman is putting the files into separate drawers.

Part ii

Sample Question

W: *Good morning, John. How are you?*
M: (A) I am fine, thank you.
M: (B) I am in the living room.
M: (C) My name is John.

21. W: *When did the conference begin?*
    M: (A) Every Tuesday.
    M: (B) An hour ago.
    M: (C) In Room 212.

22. M: *Should we drive or take the bus?*
    W: (A) There's never any place to park.
    W: (B) In the hotel at the corner.
    W: (C) To the bus stop.

23. W: *Why didn't you send in your confirmation?*
    M: (A) To the post office.
    M: (B) When I registered.
    M: (C) I changed my mind.

24. M: *How can I get tickets for the ferry?*
    W: (A) No one pays them.
    W: (B) Ten dollars one way.
    W: (C) Just go to the office.

25. W: *Have you decided if you're going to buy or rent?*
    M: (A) Turn down the air conditioner.
    M: (B) I'm not sure which is better.
    M: (C) Somewhere close to work.

26. M: *Would you mind closing the window?*
    W: (A) Yes, it's closed.
    W: (B) I'm sorry, it's too high.
    W: (C) No, it's close to the door.

27. M: *Who's responsible for paying the bills?*
    W: (A) Not me. Try the treasurer.
    W: (B) Thank you. I'm glad you got paid.
    W: (C) I take care of Bill.

28. W: *Have you raised your fees again?*
    M: (A) Not since last summer.
    M: (B) The last day of the year.
    M: (C) Employee salaries were raised last month.

29. M: *Do you jog indoors or outdoors?*
    W: (A) I like your house.
    W: (B) No, I don't.
    W: (C) I run by the pond.

30. W: *How were sales last quarter?*
    M: (A) They work until 5:00.
    M: (B) I buy retail.
    M: (C) They went up.

31. M: *When can I take my summer vacation?*
    W: (A) It's too hot in August.
    W: (B) After Kim returns on July 30.
    W: (C) At the mountains.

32. W: *You're not from Singapore, are you?*
    M: (A) No, but I live there now.
    M: (B) I sing in the shower.
    M: (C) Is it still pouring?

33. M: *Have you interviewed anyone else?*
    W: (A) Everyone will get a turn.
    W: (B) No, you're the first.
    W: (C) I can see what you mean.

34. M: *How much can my suitcases weigh?*
    W: (A) Hop on the scale.
    W: (B) Not more than sixty-five kilos.
    W: (C) Two pieces can be checked in.

35. W: *Where did the new architect used to work?*
    M: (A) In the winter.
    M: (B) The beginning of the month.
    M: (C) At our branch office.

36. M: *Is there a cafeteria in this building?*
    W: (A) Try the elevator.
    W: (B) In the basement.
    W: (C) There's a tailor on the fifth floor.

37. M: *How long should the flight take?*
    W: (A) A little over an hour.
    W: (B) About two hundred miles.
    W: (C) If it's too long, you'll trip.

38. W: *Which kind of music do you prefer, jazz or classical?*
    M: (A) That station plays only rock.
    M: (B) I often go to class.
    M: (C) I like both.

39. M: *Please fill out the forms using blue or black ink.*
    W: (A) How did the sink get so dirty?
    W: (B) How did your leg get black and blue?
    W: (C) No problem. I have a black pen.

40. W: *When did the supervisor tell our shift to take a break?*
    M: (A) What was broken?
    M: (B) Not before we finish loading.
    M: (C) Yes, we were told about the move.

41. M: *Will the paychecks be ready by 5:00?*
    W: (A) Can you check the book out for me?
    W: (B) I'll only need four.
    W: (C) They should be.

42. W: *Would you prefer I use a credit card, or pay cash for the purchase?*
    M: (A) It doesn't make any difference.
    M: (B) How long have you been waiting?
    M: (C) The bank closes soon.

43. M: *Did you enjoy the performance last night?*
    W: (A) No, Joy doesn't work at night.
    W: (B) Yes, I thought it was amazing.
    W: (C) Yes, I joined the firm some time ago.

44. W: *How far is it to the hotel from the office?*
M: (A) You can't walk there from here.
M: (B) No, it's downtown.
M: (C) No, it's closer to the airport.

45. M: *Do employees get a discount at the health club?*
W: (A) Ten thousand five hundred, not including children.
W: (B) How many do you need?
W: (C) Yes, if they're full-time.

46. W: *Why don't we go home and continue in the morning?*
M: (A) I don't know.
M: (B) Let's do that. I've had it.
M: (C) He usually gets up early.

47. M: *Let me know if you can't make the deadline.*
W: (A) Get off at the last stop.
W: (B) I didn't know the phone wasn't working.
W: (C) Everything is going right on schedule.

48. W: *Does Mr. Ramos usually return his messages?*
M: (A) Not always.
M: (B) Yes, it's a mess.
M: (C) No, he'll be back soon.

49. M: *How can I improve my typing skills?*
W: (A) Yes, you can.
W: (B) Tie it up.
W: (C) Keep practicing.

50. W: *Is the bursar's name Terry or Jerry?*
M: (A) No, he's the accountant.
M: (B) Neither. It's Kerry.
M: (C) Yes, he tore the purse.

51. W: When is the symposium supposed to be over?
M: Someone told me it should finish half an hour before the dinner.
W: Oh, do we have to stay for the dinner?

52. M: We'll need an updated resume as soon as possible.
W: Can I fax it to you?
M: No, we'd prefer you mail it.

53. M: Do you think the temporary receptionist will stay on after her two weeks are up?
W: I'm not sure, John. I heard her say she doesn't like working in a place for more than a month.
M: That's too bad. She's the best one the agency has ever sent.

54. W: I'm looking for a new computer.
M: Do you want one with a CD-ROM, and how much memory do you want?
W: Gee, I don't know. I use it only for word processing.

55. W: David, don't tell me you're being transferred.
M: Every time I start to feel at home, headquarters assigns me to a new location.
W: I hope you'll still be around for the budget negotiations.

56. M: Karen, did you fax the report to Mr. Fisher, or did you send it by overnight mail?
W: Mr. Fisher asked me to fax it, so I did yesterday about 3:00.
M: Would you call his secretary and see if it arrived?

57. M: What happens if two people from the same department want to take the same vacation week?
W: The one with seniority has priority. The policy is only one person per department per week.
M: Uh-oh. My family has a reunion planned for the last week in July.

58. W: That's the last time I drive to the airport.
M: What happened, Helmut? Did you get stuck in traffic again?
W: Not only was there a massive traffic jam, but once I got to the airport the parking lot was full.

59. M: Can you tell me how to get to the post office?
W: Go four blocks on Brattle Street. Turn right, and it's on your left.
M: I didn't realize it was so far away. Maybe I'll take a cab.

60. W: Who's in charge of maintaining the third floor copy machine?
M: I think it's Mr. Lopez. If it needs toner, I can fix it.
W: Thanks, but the paper is jammed.

61. M: How much will I have to pay to have this TV delivered?
W: We deliver for free if you live within twenty kilometers.
M: That's great, but there's no one home during the day.

62. W: All new employees need a tuberculosis test.
M: I had one two years ago. Is that OK?
W: No, it has to be within the last six months. We have free vaccinations the first Thursday of each month.

63. M: Our factory in the Philippines needs an immediate delivery of fabric dyes.
W: Will they be able to finish the Korean fabric order without them?
M: Probably not. We'd better contact every supplier in Asia.

64. W: Do you think I'd get a better rate exchanging money at a bank or at the hotel?
M: I would assume a bank, but you'd better ask.
W: OK, I'll check at the one around the corner.

65. M: I'm surprised that the research firm doesn't think the name change would be good for business.
    W: Yeah, and our team spent so long coming up with the idea.
    M: So do you think there's any chance management will still go for your suggestion?

66. W: I'll need to fly to Brussels on the tenth of next month.
    M: How long will you be staying?
    W: As long as it takes to make sure the new plant is up and running.

67. M: Any chance we can increase the advertising budget for next year?
    W: Sure there's a chance, but we'll need to see how much we spent this year.
    M: I've got some new ideas for TV ads. They may run pretty high, but they should pay off.

68. M: I need to find something to read on the plane.
    W: I can recommend the book I'm reading. It's been on the *New York Times* bestseller's list for twenty weeks.
    M: Then I'm sure the bookstore in the hotel will have it.

69. W: Did you hear we're having the banquet in the Plaza Hotel downtown?
    M: I wish we could have it on the cruise liner like last year.
    W: It was booked. Anyway, the hotel ballroom is so much more elegant.

70. W: Pablo, I just got some tickets for the outdoor concert. Do you want to come?
    M: Sorry, but I think I'd better take a rain check. I think I'm coming down with a cold.
    W: Then maybe another time.

71. W: Tom, can you join the department for dinner this evening?
    M: I'd love to. Give me five minutes while I phone home to make sure everything's OK.
    W: Sure, we won't be leaving for another fifteen minutes.

72. M: Do you have any more copies of the *International Herald Tribune?*
    W: We just sold out. Try tomorrow before noon. We have *South China Sea* from Hong Kong.
    M: Oh, so you do have other English language papers.

73. W: Shozo, do you need any help moving to your new office?
    M: I think I'm all set. The maintenance crew said they could help me this weekend.
    W: Well, let me know if I can do anything.

74. W: I'm really running behind. We have a task force meeting at noon, and I have to pick up my car by 11:30. Do you think you could get the car?
    M: No problem, Kathy. Is it at the shop on Thirty-second and Third?
    W: That's it. I'll call to tell them you're coming.

75. W: The question is should we renovate or build something new elsewhere?
    M: We shouldn't look only at the cost. This building's location is ideal, and the facade has a lot of character.
    W: Yeah, but building new will save over a million.

76. M: When was the last time the elevators were inspected?
    W: It should say inside the elevator.
    M: The certification is missing, and we could get a heavy fine if we miss the deadline.

77. W: So did you decide to take a fifteen-year fixed or a five-year variable mortgage?
    M: The bank decided for me. I had to go with the fixed.
    W: If you plan to be in your house for more than five years, I'm sure it's a better deal.

78. M: Did all the supervisors get the same pay raise?
    W: I heard everyone got the same pay raise, but that a few got bonuses.
    M: I'm sure that made a lot of people unhappy.

79. W: Any suggestion where we can get a late night snack?
    M: Why don't we try that new place around the corner?
    W: I could use some coffee if we're ever going to finish this report.

80. M: Is attendance mandatory at the Internet workshop on Wednesday evening?
    W: Maybe "mandatory" is the wrong word. Let's just say we're all expected to be there.
    M: I have so much work to do this week.

Questions 81-83 refer to the following weather report:
W: Good evening, Manila. This is Grace Chin with the Friday morning weather forecast. Today you can expect another day of rain with high winds and possible flooding in low-lying areas. The rain, which will continue all day, will be heaviest along the coast. The rain may end by Saturday afternoon, but it will remain cloudy throughout the weekend. Be careful if you're driving downtown today, for large puddles have made the traffic worse than usual. Don't forget your umbrellas, and I'll give you an update every hour on the hour.

Questions 84-86 are based on the following announcement:
M1: Attention please, shoppers. Attention please. We have a lost child, approximately three years old, on the mezzanine level. He's wearing a red shirt, navy blue shorts, and brown sandals. He has a turquoise blue backpack that says Sydney 2000 on it. We think he said his name is Jonathan. He has short, dark brown hair and is holding a small, white teddy bear. If Jonathan belongs to you, please come to the billing office on the mezzanine level as soon as possible. You can also call us from any department's phone at extension 617 to let us know you're on your way.

Questions 87-89 refer to the following introduction:

M2: Welcome to the third annual Employee of the Year luncheon. This year we are pleased to announce that Mary Lilly, our personnel director, has been selected by her colleagues and supervisors. Although Mary has been with the company only one year, in this time she has revised the employee application form, streamlined the payroll, and compiled a brochure outlining company policies and benefits for all employees. To show our appreciation, Mary is being presented with a $1,000 check, a certificate for dinner for two at Davio's Restaurant on the Waterfront, and two tickets for Sunday's Celtics' game. Please join me in a round of applause for Mary, and I hope you all enjoy your lunch.

Questions 90-92 refer to the following memo:

W: As a result of our investigation into ways of improving executive performance and making our corporation more competitive, we have decided to team up with the University of Pennsylvania's MBA program and its Executive Education Division. Instead of encouraging our executives to complete traditional degree programs, this division offers brief, needs-oriented courses offered by specialist consultants. Courses will be offered on weekends either at their campus in Philadelphia or right in our factory. After the specialists visit our facilities and meet with various employees and executives, they will devise programs tailored to our needs.

Questions 93-95 refer to this advertisement:

M2: Every day, at 36,000 feet, a global exchange of sorts takes place. Millions of freshly picked items crisscross the globe, many of them gently nestled in packaging's version of a first-class seat–a carton or container designed by Golden Star Paper Products. Whether it's Chilean grapes going to Marseilles, California melons en route to Warsaw, or Tuscan tomatoes traveling to Kyoto, what helps these items survive the trip is our package design. Last year alone our engineers designed over 44,000 distinct kinds of packaging for businesses around the world. We do it for our customers, and for all of you who crave fresh, unbruised cherries in midwinter.

Questions 96-97 refer to the following report:

M1: As of December 1, a company seeking to use popular music or lyrics, either for commercial advertising or for an in-house corporate video, will have to get permission to do so. Obtaining music permission can be done simply and cheaply by purchasing music that comes with an automatic license for use, but the choice of music available will be significantly limited. On the other hand, obtaining permission to use protected music, which includes just about any song currently available in local music stores, can be costly and lead to extensive legal procedures since the copyright laws protecting the use of current, popular music are very strict.

Questions 98-100 are based on the following news story:

W: Dogwood Technology, Inc. shares fell fifteen percent, after this maker of fax and voice message management systems said second-quarter sales and earnings would probably not meet expectations. Dogwood said that sales were lower than anticipated in the period, and that only a modest increase from the year-earlier quarter was expected. Finance chief Bob Lynch blamed continued slow demand for the company's fax equipment for the shortfall. In other news, Dogwood acquired Telecom Inc. for eleven million dollars in cash. The move gives Dogwood a line of network interface cards, which allow networked computers and servers to communicate with the outside world.

ANSWERS & EXPLANATIONS TEST ONE

Part i

1. (B) *The woman is holding some files in her hands.*
   Choice (A) is incorrect because they are outside; there are cars on the street. Choice (C) is incorrect because they are not in a car waiting in traffic; they are standing on the sidewalk. Choice (D) is incorrect because they are talking to each other and not waiting to cross the street.

2. (D) *The door on the left is open, while the door on the right is closed.*
   Choice (A) is incorrect because the door on the left is open. Choice (B) is incorrect because the decoration is hanging between the two doors. Choice (C) is incorrect because there are no people in the picture.

3. (A) *The woman is sewing a large, heavy object, most probably a coat.*
   Choice (B) is incorrect because the woman is still working. Choice (C) is incorrect because the machine is already on. Choice (D) is incorrect because the woman is sewing the garment, not measuring it.

4. (B) *The man has the receiver to his ear and is listening to someone.*
   Choice (A) is incorrect because he is not hanging up the phone. Choice (C) is incorrect because the man is not speaking; he is listening. Choice (D) is incorrect because he is listening on the phone, so it has been installed.

5. (C) *The suitcase is open; there are some items already in the suitcase, and the woman is placing more items into the bag.*
   Choice (A) is incorrect because the woman is at home and not at the airport. Choice (B) is incorrect because the suitcase is not on a scale. Choice (D) is incorrect because the woman is still packing.

6. (D) *The doctors are looking at a file.*
   Choice (A) is incorrect because the doctor on the left, wearing a stethoscope, is looking at a file. Choice (B) is incorrect because they are standing in a room, not entering one. Choice (C) is incorrect because the doctors are not writing anything.

7. (B) *The woman on the left is looking at her monitor.*
   Choice (A) is incorrect because two women are working behind the desk. Choice (C) is incorrect because the women are behind the counter. Choice (D) is incorrect because there are no customers in the picture.

8. (A) *The restaurant is empty and the tables are set, awaiting diners.*
   Choice (B) is incorrect because there are no waiters in the picture. Choice (C) is incorrect because no food is being served. Choice (D) is incorrect because no one is in the picture.

9. (C) *The men are similarly dressed, wearing uniforms, marching in a parade.*
   Choice (A) is incorrect because only a few spectators can be seen. Choice (B) is incorrect because six men are in the front line, but only three flags are in view. Choice (D) is incorrect because the men are marching in a straight line in the same direction.

10. (B) *Several boats, rowers, and passengers are in clear view.*
    Choice (A) is incorrect because the boats are on the water, not at the dock. Choice (C) is incorrect because several people can be seen rowing. Choice (D) is incorrect because the water is calm.

11. (D) *The fruits and vegetables are on a blanket outside on the ground.*
    Choice (A) is incorrect because there are no visible prices. Choice (B) is incorrect because although there is a scale in the picture, no produce is on it. Choice (C) is incorrect because they are on a blanket, not on a table.

12. (A) *There is a car to the left of the building and cars to the right of the building.*
    Choice (B) is incorrect because the building is six stories high. Choice (C) is incorrect because there is no construction blocking the view of the building. Choice (D) is incorrect because there are no taller buildings next to the one in view.

13. (C) *There are tall trees on both sides of the street.*
    Choice (A) is incorrect because there is only one car in the picture. Choice (B) is incorrect because there is an approaching car. Choice (D) is incorrect because there are only two lanes on the road.

14. (C) *The man and woman are riding on the same bicycle.*
    Choice (A) is incorrect because the woman is riding with the man, not waving to him. Choice (B) is incorrect because the woman is behind the man. Choice (D) is incorrect because the man is not waving.

15. (A) *The women are looking into a shop window.*
    Choice (B) is incorrect because it confuses washing the window with watching something. Choice (C) is incorrect because the women are not inside the window, working on a display. Choice (D) is incorrect because they are not replacing the window.

16. (B) *The boy's leg is in the air and the ball is in front of it; he has just kicked it.*
    Choice (A) is incorrect because he is kicking, not throwing the ball. Choice (C) is incorrect because no one is catching the ball. Choice (D) is incorrect because the ball is in the air.

17. (D) *People are looking at paintings displayed at an outdoor market.*
    Choice (A) is incorrect because no one is painting in the picture. Choice (B) is incorrect because the paintings are outside, not at a museum. Choice (C) is incorrect because the paintings are not inside a building on a wall.

18. (D) *The baby is in a stroller, being pushed by the father.*
Choice (A) is incorrect because the father is pushing the baby, the mother isn't. Choice (B) is incorrect because the baby is in a stroller. Choice (C) is incorrect because the parents are walking, not riding motorcycles.

19. (C) *The man and woman are walking with their arms intertwined.*
Choice (A) is incorrect because the man's arm is not on the woman's shoulder. Choice (B) is incorrect because the couple is walking together; she is not carrying him. Choice (D) is incorrect because the man and woman are walking together.

20. (B) *The woman is checking her files.*
Choice (A) is incorrect because the folders are on the woman's lap, not on her desk. Choice (C) is incorrect because she is not writing on the files; she's looking at them. Choice (D) is incorrect because she is not putting her files into drawers.

21. (B) *An hour ago* answers *when* the conference began.
Choice (A) answers *how often*, not *when*. Choice (C) answers *where*.

22. (A) *There's never any place to park* means the speaker thinks they should take the bus and not drive because they won't find a parking space.
Choice (B) answers a *where* question. Choice (C) repeats the word *bus* but answers *where*.

23. (C) *I changed my mind* explains *why* the speaker didn't *send in the confirmation.*
Choice (A) answers *where*, not *why*. Choice (B) answers *When did you send?* not *Why didn't you send?*

24. (C) *Just go to the office* means tickets are sold at the office.
Choice (A) refers to *people* not being paid. Choice (B) answers the question *How much are the tickets?*

25. (B) *I'm not sure which is better* shows the speaker hasn't decided yet whether to *buy* or *rent*.
Choice (A) is an illogical response. Choice (C) answers the question *Where are you going to live?*

26. (B) *I'm sorry, it's too high* means the speaker is unable to reach the window to close it.
Choice (A) confuses *closed* with *closing* and answers the question *Is the window closed?* Choice (C) confuses *close* with *closing* and corrects a statement such as *Is ___ close to the window?*

27. (A) *Not me. Try the treasurer* means the speaker isn't responsible for paying the bills and suggests asking someone else.
Choice (B) is illogical and confuses *paid* with *paying*. Choice (C) confuses the man's name *Bill* with *bills*.

28. (A) *Not since last summer* answers the question about whether or not the fees have been raised again; his response means *yes, but not recently.*
Choice (B) answers *when* fees were raised, not *if*. Choice (C) answers a question about employee salaries, not fees.

29. (C) *I run by the pond* means that the speaker runs *outdoors*.
Choice (A) is an illogical response. Choice (B) answers *Do you jog?*

30. (C) *They went up* answers *how sales were;* it means sales were better.
Choice (A) answers *until what time* people work. Choice (B) answers *Do you buy retail or wholesale?*

31. (B) *After Kim returns on July 30* means the man can take his vacation any time after Kim's.
Choice (A) answers the question *Should I take my vacation in August?* Choice (C) answers *where* to take a vacation.

32. (A) *No, but I live there now* indicates that the man lives there now but is from somewhere else originally.
Choice (B) confuses *sing* with *Singapore*. Choice (C) confuses *pouring* with *Singapore*.

33. (B) *No, you're the first* answers whether anyone else has been interviewed.
Choice (A) would be said to someone not being given a chance to speak. Choice (C) is illogical and would be a response to a statement, not a question.

34. (B) *Not more than sixty-five kilos* answers how much his suitcases are allowed to weigh.
Choice (A) would be said to a person who wants to weigh him/herself; a suitcase can't hop. Choice (C) answers *How many pieces of luggage are allowed?*

35. (C) *At our branch office* tells where the new architect used to work.
Choice (A) answers a *when* question. Choice (B) also answers a *when* question.

36. (B) *In the basement* gives a logical location for where in the building a cafeteria would be.
Choices (A) and (C) are illogical responses.

37. (A) *A little over an hour* tells *how long the flight should take.*
Choice (B) answers *how long the flying distance is,* not *how long it takes*. Choice (C) confuses *long* with *how long* and *trip*, a word related to *flight*.

38. (C) *I like both* answers *which kind of music* the speaker prefers.
Choice (A) answers *which kind of music* a radio station plays. Choice (B) confuses *class* and *classical*.

39. (C) *No problem, I have a black pen* is a suitable response to being told to use either *blue or black ink*.
Choice (A) confuses *sink* with *ink*. Choice (B) confuses *black and blue bruises* with *black and blue ink*.

40. (B) *Not before we finish loading* answers when a supervisor told employees to take a break.
Choice (A) confuses *broken* (not working) with *break* (a pause). Choice (C) uses *told*, the same verb as the question, but this response does not answer *when*.

41. (C) *They should be* indicates that the checks will probably be ready by 5:00.
Choice (A) confuses *check out a book* with *checks*. Choice (B) confuses the number *four* with *5:00*.

42. (A) *It doesn't make any difference* answers that paying by credit card or by cash are both the same.
Choice (B) is an illogical question in response to the preference question. Choice (C) confuses *bank* with finance words, *credit card* and *pay cash*.

43. (B) *Yes, I thought it was amazing* shows that the speaker thoroughly enjoyed the performance.
Choice (A) confuses the woman's name *Joy* with *enjoy*. Choice (C) confuses *enjoy* with *joined*.

44. (A) *You can't walk there from here* tells that the distance of one building from the other is too far to walk.
Choices (B) and (C) do not answer *how far*.

45. (C) *Yes, if they're full-time* answers whether employees get a discount at the health club by qualifying *which employees*.
Choice (A) answers *how many*. Choice (B) answers with an illogical question.

46. (B) *Let's do that* means I'd like to, and responds to the suggestion *Why don't we? I've had it* means *I'm tired*.
Choices (A) and (C) are illogical responses to the suggestion.

47. (C) *Everything is going right on schedule* indicates that she'll be able to *make the deadline*.
Choice (A) responds to *let me know where* to get off a bus or train. Choice (B) is an illogical response.

48. (A) *Not always* answers whether or not *Mr. Ramos usually returns his messages*.
Choice (B) confuses *mess* with *messages*. Choice (C) confuses *be back* with *return messages*.

49. (C) *Keep practicing* tells the speaker *how* he can improve his typing.
Choice (A) does not answer *how*. Choice (B) confuses *tie* and *typing*.

50. (B) *Neither. It's Kerry* answers what the bursar's name is.
Choice (A) answers the question *Is Terry the bursar?* Choice (C) confuses *tore* with *Terry*.

51. (B) The symposium will finish *half an hour before the dinner*.
Choices (A) and (C) are not accurate. Choice (D) confuses *half an hour* in length with dinner being served *half an hour* after the symposium.

52. (C) The man says *we'd prefer you mail* the resume.
Choice (A) is incorrect — although the woman asks if she can *fax* her resume, he says no. Choices (B) and (D) are contradicted by the fact that the means of delivery should be through the mail.

53. (A) The man says *she's the best one the agency has ever sent,* which means the same as *so far*.
Choice (B) is incorrrect — he is very happy with her work. Although her assignment is for two weeks. Choice (C) is incorrect because he would like her to work more than two weeks. Choice (D) is incorrect because she doesn't like staying in a place more than a month, not that she *doesn't like temporary jobs*.

54. (D) She says she only uses the computer for *word processing*.
Choice (A) is not mentioned. Choice (B) confuses *to increase memory* with asking *how much memory she wants*. The salesperson asks her if she'd like a computer with a CD-ROM but she answers *I don't know*, making Choice (C) incorrect.

55. (C) The man will be *assigned to a new location*.
In Choice (A), the woman hopes he'll *still be around for budget negotiations*, but that doesn't explain his transfer. Choice (B) is not mentioned. In Choice (D), *headquarters* made the decision, but he will not be working there.

56. (D) The woman says *she faxed the report yesterday about 3:00,* so Mr. Fisher should have it by now.
Choices (A) is incorrect because Karen faxed it; she didn't mail it. Choice (B) is incorrect because Karen says she faxed it yesterday. Choice (C) is incorrect because the fax is with Mr. Fisher, not on Karen's desk.

57. (A) *The one with seniority has priority* means the person who has been working longer can take the vacation week if two people want the same week.
Choices (B), (C), and (D) are contradicted by the statement *the one with seniority*.

58. (C) *Once I got to the airport the parking lot was full* means he could not find a place to park.
Choice (A) is incorrect — he does not mention or imply that he missed his flight. Choice (B) is incorrect. He was in a traffic *jam*, not a traffic *accident*. Choice (D) is incorrect because he was *in* a traffic jam; however, he didn't *cause* one.

59. (B) *Go four blocks on Brattle Street, turn right, and it's on your left.*
Choice (A) is incorrect because getting to the post office involves turning right onto a different street. Choice (C) is incorrect because the post office is *on your left.* Choice (D) is not mentioned.

60. (D) The woman says *the paper is jammed.*
The man says he can fix the machine *if it needs toner,* Choice (A), but he's told *the paper is jammed.* Choice (B) confuses *maintenance* with *maintaining.* Choice (C) is not mentioned.

61. (A) The man says *but there's no one home during the day.*
Choice (B) is incorrect; *That's great* shows that he does live within the delivery radius. Choice (C) is incorrect; he has already chosen a TV. Choice (D) is contradicted by *we deliver for free.*

62. (B) The vaccinations are given *the first Thursday of each month* which means *one time per month.*
Choice (A) is not mentioned. Choice (C) confuses *the first Thursday of each month* with *every Thursday.* Choice (D) confuses *two years ago* with *every two years.*

63. (D) The Philippine factory needs an immediate delivery of *fabric dyes.*
Choice (A) is incorrect; what is needed is the fabric *dyes,* not fabric *factories.* Choice (B) is incorrect; no contact person is mentioned. The *order for Korea* does not need to be located, the *dyes to make the orders* do. Therefore, Choice (C) is incorrect.

64. (C) The woman wants to know if she'd *get a better rate exchanging money at a bank or at the hotel.*
She doesn't ask which bank the man uses, so Choice (A) is incorrect. She doesn't need to know where a bank is, so Choice (D) is incorrect. Choice (B) is not mentioned.

65. (B) The woman says *our team spent so long coming up with the idea* (for the name change).
Choice (A) is incorrect; management may consider the change. Choice (C) is incorrect; the research firm didn't like the idea of the name change. Choice (D) is not mentioned.

66. (A) The man says he'll be in Brussels *as long as it takes to make sure the plant is up and running,* which means *until the plant is operational.*
He is *leaving on the tenth,* so Choice (B) is incorrect. Choices (C) and (D) are not mentioned.

67. (D) The man says he's *got some new ideas for TV ads.*
The woman mentions Choice (A). Choices (B) and (C) are not mentioned.

68. (C) The man, upon hearing of the woman's book recommendation, says he's *sure the bookstore in the hotel will have it.*
Choice (A) is not mentioned; it is likely he will look for and buy the recommended book. Choice (B) confuses reading the *New York Times* newspaper with the *New York Times* bestseller's list of *books.* Choice (D) is not mentioned or implied.

69. (A) The man says the banquet was on a *cruise liner last year* and the woman asks if he's heard that this year's will be *in the Plaza Hotel downtown.*
Choice (B) is incorrect; it was on board a ship last year. Choice (C) is incorrect; it should be more elegant than last year's. Choice (D) is not mentioned.

70. (B) Pablo says he thinks he's *coming down with a cold,* meaning he doesn't feel well.
Choice (A) confuses *raining* with *a rain check,* meaning *postpone until a later time.* Choice (C) confuses *having a cold* and *being cold.* Choice (D) confuses *check* and *rain check.*

71. (D) Tom says he needs five minutes to *phone home to make sure everything's OK.*
Choice (A) is incorrect because they'll be *leaving* in fifteen minutes; Tom only asks them to wait *five* minutes. In Choice (B) there may be confusion between the words *phone home* and *go home.* Tom wants to make sure everything's OK at *home,* not at the *office,* Choice (C).

72. (A) The man is told that the paper he wants is *sold out* and that he should *try tomorrow before noon.*
Choice (B) is incorrect; the paper is sold there, but all of the papers have been sold. Choice (C) is not mentioned. Choice (D) is incorrect; there is at least another English paper for sale there, but not the one the man requests.

73. (C) When asked if he needs any help moving, Shozo replies he thinks he's *all set,* meaning *everything is OK.*
Choices (A), (B), and (D) are not mentioned.

74. (B) Kathy is speaking to someone at work, a *colleague,* because she refers to a *meeting at noon.*
Kathy will *call* the mechanic, Choice (A). There are no indications that she's talking to either Choice (C) or (D).

75. (D) The woman says *building new will save over a million.*
Building a new building would not include renovating and maintaining the facade, so Choice (A) is incorrect. A new building would be built *elsewhere,* so Choice (B) is incorrect. Choice (C) is not mentioned.

76. (A) Because the woman says *it should say inside the elevator,* it is understood they are not inside the elevator when they are talking.
Therefore Choice (B) is incorrect. Choice (C) is not mentioned. Choice (D) confuses *inspector* and *inspected.*

77. (D) The man says *the bank decided for me; I had to go with the fixed* (mortgage).
The woman says *it's a better deal,* Choice (A), but the man didn't *choose* it. Choice (B) is not mentioned. Choice (C) is incorrect; the man does not indicate when he plans to move.

78. (C) The woman says *a few (of the supervisors) got bonuses.*
Choice (A) is incorrect although all the supervisors received pay raises. Choice (B) is contradicted by the fact only *a few* got bonuses. Choice (D) is incorrect; those who received bonuses also received pay raises.

79. (B) The woman asks *where they can get a snack,* meaning *where they can get something to eat.*
Choice (A) is incorrect because they are not discussing restaurant locations, but rather where to find one that is open. Choices (C) and (D) are not mentioned.

80. (A) The man says he has *so much work to do this week* and asks if his attendance is *mandatory,* implying he does not want to go.
Choice (B) is not mentioned. Choice (C) is incorrect; he does not imply that he will not attend. He only implies he doesn't want to attend. Choice (D) is incorrect because he asks about the meeting *on Wednesday evening.*

81. (B) The woman is presenting the *Friday* morning forecast. Therefore Choices (A), (C), and (D) are contradicted by *Friday.*

82. (C) *Today you can expect another day of rain,* which means *continued rain.*
Choice (A) is not mentioned. Choice (B) is incorrect because the rain *may not end until Saturday afternoon.* Choice (D) is incorrect because there will be *high winds.*

83. (D) The woman says *Don't forget your umbrellas.*
She says to *be careful if you're driving today*; she's not saying *not to drive,* Choice (A). Choice (B) is incorrect, although she says rain will be heaviest in coastal areas. Choice (C) is not mentioned.

84. (A) The announcement begins *Attention please shoppers,* so it must be in a department store.
Choices (B), (C), and (D) are not mentioned.

85. (C) The announcement says *we have a lost child on the mezzanine level.*
The child is *lost,* not *with his parents,* so Choice (A) is incorrect. Choices (B) and (D) are contradicted by *in the billing office.*

86. (D) The parents are told to *please come to the billing office* or to *call (the office) from any phone.*
Choice (A) confuses *bill* with *billing office.* Choices (B) and (C) are contradicted by *come to* or *call the billing office.*

87. (B) *Welcome to the third annual Employee of the Year luncheon.*
Choice (A) confuses *waterfront* with the certificate Mary Lilly receives for *Davio's Restaurant on the Waterfront.* Choice (C) confuses the place of the introduction with the restaurant for which Mary receives a certificate. Choice (D) is contradicted by *luncheon.*

88. (A) The introduction says *Mary Lilly, our personnel director.*
Choices (B), (C), and (D) are contradicted by *our personnel director,* jobs *not* performed by someone in this position.

89. (C) *Mary has been with the company only one year.*
Choices (A), (B), and (D) are contradicted by this information.

90. (D) It says *as a result of our investigation into ways of improving executive performance,* so that is the corporation goal.
Choice (A) is incorrect; Philadelphia is only mentioned as the location of the campus. Choice (B) is incorrect because *specialists will devise programs,* not *executives.* Choice (C) is incorrect because the corporation is offering *needs-oriented courses* rather than *traditional degree programs.*

91. (A) *This division offers brief courses.*
Choice (B) is incorrect because the courses are offered *in Philadelphia* or *in our factory,* which may be outside of Philadelphia. Choice (C) is not mentioned. Choice (D) is incorrect because *courses will be offered on weekends.*

92. (B) The courses are *offered by specialist consultants.*
Choices (A) and (D) are incorrect because the courses will be *taken* by executives and employees. Choice (C) confuses *tailored to our needs (on our needs)* with *tailors.*

93. (C) Golden Star has *over 44,000 kinds of packaging.*
Choice (A) compares the comfort and safety of their packaging to a *first-class seat (on an airplane).* Although various fruits *(melons and grapes)* are mentioned as the contents of the packages, Choice (B) is incorrect. Golden Star employs *engineers,* but Choice (D) is contradicted by *packaging.*

94. (D) *Every day at 36,000 feet* implies the packages are sent by air.
At 36,000 feet contradicts Choices (A) and (C). The cargo travels in *packaging's version of a first-class seat,* but no mention is made of the cargo traveling in the first-class section, so Choice (B) is incorrect.

95. (C) The advertisement states that *last year alone our engineers designed over 44,000 distinct kinds of packaging.*
Choices (A), (B), and (D) are contradicted by *44,000.*

96. (B) *As of December 1, a company seeking to use popular music for advertising will have to get permission.*
Choice (A) is incorrect; the report does not discuss popular music becoming protected. Choice (C) is incorrect; it only states that copyright laws protecting the use of popular music are strict. Choice (D) is not mentioned.

97. (A) The report states that *protected music can be costly.*
Choices (B) and (C) are incorrect because *obtaining (popular) music permission can be done... cheaply by purchasing music that comes with an automatic license.* Choice (D) is incorrect because the report discusses only obtaining music permission.

98. (D) Dogwood Technology is a *maker of fax and voice message management systems.*
Choice (A) is not mentioned. Choice (B) confuses *telephone* with the company Dogwood acquired, Telecom. Choice (C) is incorrect; they are only mentioned in relation to the acquisition of Telecom.

99. (C) The *shares fell fifteen percent.*
Choice (A) confuses *two percent* with *second-quarter.* Choice (B) confuses *eleven percent* with *eleven million dollars.* Choice (D) is not mentioned.

100. (B) *Bob Lynch blamed continued slow demand for the company's fax equipment for the shortfall.*
The slow demand for *fax equipment* contradicts Choice (A). Choices (C) and (D) are not reasons for the shortfall.

101. (A) The relationship between these two independent clauses is one of opposition, so *but* is the correct conjunction.
Choice (B) would introduce part of an independent clause and needs to be paired with *or.* Choice (C) is illogical, as it introduces a result. Choice (D), a non-restrictive relative clause pronoun referring to things, not people, usually follows a noun.

102. (C) One *makes* spreadsheets.
Choices (A), (B), and (D) are not used with the word *spreadsheets.*

103. (D) *Apt* meaning *likely* is the only word that completes this sentence correctly.
Choice (A), *no,* is used either as a refusal or preceding a noun. Choice (B) is a modal that cannot follow *is.* Choice (C) is either a verb, and therefore cannot follow *is,* or a preposition, preceding a noun.

104. (B) The superlative form of the adjective, *smallest,* follows *the.*
Choice (A) is the simple form of the adjective. Choice (C) is the comparative form. Choice (D) is a different simple form of the adjective.

105. (D) Only a person, such as a *colleague,* meaning *associate,* can be *educated.*
Choice (A) is a noun thing. Choice (B) is an adjective. Choice (C) is a noun thing.

106. (A) *Over* is a preposition that can be used with amounts to mean *more than.*
Choice (B) means *smaller than* and would be illogical. Choices (C) and (D) indicate location.

107. (C) *Consideration* means *careful thought,* and is the only logical choice.
Choice (A) means *agreement among things or parts.* Choice (B) means *the act of offering comfort.* Choice (D) means *preservation from loss, damage, or neglect.*

108. (B) The passive form of the verb *be made* is needed in this sentence.
Choice (A) is the active present tense. Choice (C) is the active past. Choice (D), although passive, cannot follow *must.*

109. (A) The adjective form *increasing* follows the article and precedes the noun.
Choices (B) and (C) are either verbs or nouns. Choice (D) is an adverb.

110. (D) *Go in on,* a phrasal verb, means *contribute to.*
Choice (A) means *take care of.* Choice (B) means *surrender.* Choice (C) is illogical.

111. (C) One can *reduce* the amount of *paperwork* by using *direct deposits,* a way to deposit paychecks.
Although Choices (A), (B), and (D) are all nouns and are correct grammatically, they are not logical in this sentence.

112. (A) The adverb *seldom* modifies the verb *include.*
Choice (B), although an adverb, is used only with questions and negative sentences. Choice (C) is an adjective. Choice (D), although an adverb, is frequently used to describe adjectives, as in *unusually hot.*

113. (C) In this context, only *requires* is the appropriate verb.
Choices (A), (B), and (D) are not logical.

114. (B) After the preposition *for,* an object pronoun is needed.
Choice (A) is a possessive pronoun. Choices (C) and (D) are subject pronouns.

115. (A) The correct word order in this passive causative clause is the helping verb, *had;* direct object, *his office;* past participle, *redecorated.*
In choices (B), (C), and (D), the word order is illogical.

116. (C) *Take steps* is an idiom which means that procedures have been implemented.
Choices (A), (B), and (D) are not logical.

117. (D) The preposition *during* means *throughout or over time.*
Choice (A) indicates location *at the back of.* Choice (B) indicates location *at the side of.* Choice (C) indicates location *from the other side of.*

118. (B) The adjective *confident* means *sure of,* and is the only logical choice.
Choice (A) means *real.* Choice (C) means *awake.* Choice (D) means *uninterrupted.*

119. (A) The adverb *widely* means *very* or *in many places* and modifies *popular.*
Choice (B) is a noun. Choices (C) and (D) are adjectives.

120. (D) The correct word order is preposition, *prior to;* article, *the;* adverbial phrase, *March first;* noun, *deadline.*
In choices (A), (B), and (C), the word order is illogical.

121. (C) The verb *tend* is followed by an infinitive, *to keep*.
Choice (A) is a preposition with the gerund form. Choice (B) is the passive infinitive form. Choice (D) is a gerund.

122. (B) *With breakfast afterwards* means that breakfast will be after the orientation.
Choice (A) is an adjective which cannot follow the noun. Choice (C), which can be an adverb, means *frontward*. Choice (D), which can be an adverb, means *with*.

123. (B) *Access to over four hundred pages* means *more than four hundred pages*.
Choice (A) means *past* or *in the distance*. Choices (C) and (D) need to be followed by *than* to be grammatically correct.

124. (A) *Make decisions immediately* means *decide without delay*.
Choice (B) is usually an adjective. Choices (C) and (D) are illogical in this time frame; *make* is present, so *yesterday*, which indicates the past, and *shortly*, which means *soon*, cannot be used.

125. (C) The expression *to stay in touch with* is an idiom meaning *remain in contact with*.
Therefore, Choices (A), (B), and (D) are incorrect.

126. (D) *As well as* indicates an additional point and since *sales* were *strong, as well as consistent revenue* is a logical positive addition.
Choice (A) means *including a promise*. Choice (B) is not used with *revenue*. Choice (C) means *descending*.

127. (A) *Provided by a bank* means *supplied*, and is the only logical choice.
Choice (B) has several meanings; the most common is *raise someone else's baby as one's own*. Choice (C) means *replaced*. Choice (D) means *told in advance what would happen*.

128. (B) *Remains in effect* means *stays valid*, and is the only logical choice.
Choice (A) means *strength*. Choice (C) means *an amount for a given use*. Choice (D) means *honor*.

129. (B) *No heat or humidity* explains that heat and humidity keep computers from functioning optimally.
Choice (A) cannot follow *almost*. Choice (C) is a pronoun and cannot precede a noun. Choice (D) cannot follow *almost*, and cannot be paired with *or*.

130. (C) A *letter of resignation* informs a company that one is quitting.
Choice (A) means *memory*. Choice (B) means *a result produced by an action*. Choice (D) means *time spent in recovery*.

131. (D) *Whom* is a relative pronoun used with people, as with *the treasurer*.
Choice (A) is a relative pronoun that refers to things. Choice (B) is an object pronoun, not a relative pronoun. Choice (C) is not a relative pronoun.

132. (A) *Upright* means *in a vertical position*.
Choices (B), (C), and (D) do not refer to direction.

133. (C) *Negotiated* means *settled by discussion and agreement*, and is the only logical choice.
Choice (A) means *twisted out of shape*. Choice (B) means *given in abundance*. Choice (D) means *became more forgiving*.

134. (B) *In contrast to* indicates opposition.
Choice (A) must be followed by a noun or noun clause. Choice (C) introduces an explanation, not a contrast. Choice (D) must be followed by a subject and a verb.

135. (D) *Unlike,* a preposition followed by the noun *faxes*, indicates that a contrast follows.
Choice (A) is an adverb. Choice (B) is a verb. Choice (C) is either an adjective or an adverb which is used to show similarity.

136. (D) *Have adopted direct marketing as* means *utilized*.
Choice (A) does not work with *as a means of*. Choices (B) and (C) are not logical.

137. (A) *Since the 1990's* indicates that the present perfect *has been* is needed.
Choice (B) is the simple past. Choice (C) is the simple past + infinitive. Choice (D) is an incorrect verb form.

138. (C) *Range* means vary, and is the only logical choice.
Choice (A) means *change in position*. Choice (B) means *move from one place to another*. Choice (D) means *surround*.

139. (C) *Rely on* means *depend on*.
Choices (A), (B), and (D) are not used with *rely*.

140. (B) *Spur* means *incentive*, and is the only logical choice.
Choice (A) means *fee*. Choice (C) means *valuable stone*. Choice (D) means *turning away from the main subject*.

141. (C) The superlative is incorrect; the adjective form *short* or the comparative *shorter* should be used.

142. (B) *Totally and completely* gives the same information and is redundant; one word or the other should be used.

143. (B) *They* is not necessary because the sentence already has a subject — *negotiators*.

144. (D) *Accommodations* refers to lodging and is always plural.

145. (D) In a compound noun, the first noun should not be possessive — *highway construction.*

146. (A) The expression *in the 1970's* requires the simple past tense here — *were.*

147. (C) *Using* introduces a modifying phrase, which makes this sentence parallel.

148. (D) The noun *marketing* should precede the noun *consultant* to make a compound noun.

149. (D) *Matinee* means daytime performance; therefore, *daytime* makes the expression redundant.

150. (B) *Method* is a singular noun, and therefore takes a singular verb — *helps.*

151. (B) The passive form of the verb is needed — *marketed.*

152. (A) *Founded,* the past participle from a reduced adjective clause, should be used.

153. (D) This error is one of word choice; *from throughout the world* is correct. The preposition *through* means *in one side and out the other.*

154. (C) The plural form *bills* is needed to agree with *they.*

155. (C) The verb form *has cut* keeps the sentence parallel.

156. (B) *Either... or* is a paired conjunction — *either create or purchase.*

157. (D) Use the person form *architects* to make the phrase parallel — *by psychologists and architects.*

158. (A) The participle form of the verb is needed to make a correct passive form — *can be rented.*

159. (A) The correct expression is *to take a poll.*

160. (C) When a clause begins with *there,* the verb agrees with the noun which comes after it — *there are no interviews.*

Part vii

161. (C) It promises *to be this country's most luxurious shopping center.*
Choices (A), (B), and (D) are not mentioned.

162. (B) The mall will open its *ten floors* for business.
Choice (A) confuses *eight theaters* with *ten floors.* Choice (C) confuses *twenty restaurants* with *ten floors.* Choice (D) confuses *one hundred* boutiques with *ten floors.*

163. (C) A *symposium* is an *exposition.*
Choice (A) is confusing because although the symposium will benefit *your company and your career,* it is not a place to find a job. Choices (B) and (D) are not mentioned.

164. (D) World Workplace is where professionals meet to discuss ideas involved *with providing an effective work environment.*
Choices (A) and (C) are not mentioned. Choice (B) is incorrect because although the symposium will *benefit your career,* there is no mention of *new possibilities.*

165. (A) *Interior design* is not mentioned.
Choices (B), (C), and (D) are explicitly mentioned.

166. (B) The new nonstop flights from Detroit *make it easier than ever for you to keep up with Asia's transformation,* so flights are to Asia.
Choice (A) is incorrect because flights are from the east coast and southeast. Choice (C) is incorrect because flights originating from the east coast stop in either Minneapolis/St. Paul or Detroit before leaving for Asia. Choice (D) is not mentioned.

167. (C) *Connecting in St. Paul can save you up to four hours from the east coast.*
Choices (A) and (B) are not mentioned. Choice (D) is contradicted by *connecting in St. Paul.*

168. (C) *By credit card* is not mentioned.
Choices (A), (B), and (D) are explicitly mentioned.

169. (B) *If you think your bill is wrong, write us at the address printed on your statement.*
Choice (A) is contradicted by *you are still obligated to pay the part of the bill not in question.* Choice (C) is not mentioned. Choice (D) is mentioned as something *not* to do: *please do not telephone us.*

170. (D) *You are still obligated to pay the part of the bill not in question.*
Choice (A) is contradicted by *you do not have to pay any amount in question.* Choices (B) and (C) are contradicted by *pay the part of the bill not in question.*

171. (B) *The annual meeting... will be held* informs the trustees of the upcoming meeting.
Choice (A) is mentioned but is not the main purpose of the announcement. Choices (C) and (D) are not mentioned.

172. (D) *Finance* is one of the three new programs being considered.
Choices (A) *physical education* and (C) *occupational therapy* are confused by the new program *physical therapy*. Choice (B) is not mentioned.

173. (A) The meeting will be held *prior to the commencement ceremony*, so commencement will be held *after the meeting*.
Choices (B), (C), and (D) are contradicted by *prior to the commencement ceremony*.

174. (D) *International calls, operators,* and *cellular phones* suggest a *phone service* company.
Choices (A), (B), and (C) are not mentioned.

175. (B) A one-minute call to Egypt costs seventy-five cents, so a ten-minute call would cost $7.50.
Choices (A), (C), and (D) are contradicted by the cost for a one-minute call to Egypt.

176. (D) If one saves up to eighty percent on all international calls, one would be saving money on rates.
Choices (A), (B), and (C) are not mentioned.

177. (A) If one receives twenty-seven issues in six months, then at least four magazines arrive monthly.
Choice (B) is contradicted by the cost of twelve months at seventy-nine cents per copy, while the cost for twenty-four months is sixty-nine cents per copy. Choice (C) is contradicted by the option to *bill me later*. Choice (D) is contradicted by the renewal option.

178. (B) *Attach label* appears next to *renewal*.
Choices (A), (C), and (D) are contradicted by *attach label*.

179. (C) Subscription for twenty-four months is sixty-nine cents per copy, the cheapest per copy, so it's the best value.
Choices (A) and (B) are seventy-nine cents per copy. Choice (D) is not a subscription length offered.

180. (D) WalkFit is not an *ordinary walking machine*, so it's *an exercise machine*.
Choices (A) and (B) are contradicted by *ordinary walking machine*. Choice (C) is contradicted by *WalkFit's arm exerciser*.

181. (A) *Cost* is not mentioned.
Choices (B), (C), and (D) are explicitly mentioned.

182. (B) One hour on WalkFit *burns an average of 850 calories* which is *twice as many calories as motorized treadmills*, so a motorized treadmill burns 425 calories.
Choices (A), (C), and (D) are contradicted by *burns an average of 850 calories*, which is *twice as many calories as motorized treadmills*.

183. (D) *Just 30 minutes, 4 times a week is all it takes*, so *120 minutes* is recommended.
Choices (A), (B), and (C) are contradicted by the statement *Just 30 minutes, 4 times a week is all it takes.*

184. (D) *Ordinary walking machines simply can't exercise your whole body.*
Choices (A) and (B) are not mentioned. Choice (C) is incorrect because the upper body is not the *only* area of focus.

185. (C) *This is not just a globe, but a three-dimensional computerized atlas.*
Choice (A) is contradicted by *three-dimensional.* Choices (B) and (D) are not mentioned.

186. (B) *Touch any country with a special pointer.*
Choices (A), (C), and (D) are contradicted by *with a special pointer.*

187. (C) *The Metropolis cartridge provides facts on over five hundred cities.*
Choices (A), (B), and (D) are contradicted by *the Metropolis cartridge provides facts on over five hundred cities.*

188. (A) *The Information Please Business Almanac offers a variety of resources for free.*
Choice (B) is not mentioned. Choice (C) is contradicted by *The Business Almanac may add new items periodically.* Choice (D) is contradicted by the instruction to write to the *Business Almanac if you have questions or comments.* The documents are received by e-mail.

189. (D) *You should receive your document within a few seconds or minutes depending on the type of service you are using.*
Choices (A), (B), and (C) are not mentioned in connection with the time it takes to receive a message.

190. (B) *Simply send a message to one of the addresses listed below the instructions.*
Choices (A), (C), and (D) are contradicted by *simply send a message to one of the addresses listed below the instructions.*

191. (D) *Both (ships) have been awarded six stars.*
Choice (A) is incorrect; they are of different sizes. Choice (B) is incorrect; only *Empire Diamond's* twin hull is mentioned. Choice (C) is incorrect because the crew-to-guest ratio is only mentioned in relation to *Song of Emeralds.*

192. (A) The ships sail *from early May through October*, six months.
Choices (B), (C), and (D) are contradicted by the statement *from early May through October.*

193. (D) *Its innovative twin hull* is not mentioned.
Choices (A), (B), and (C) are explicitly mentioned.

194. (D) *Whether you're completing your bachelor's degree or preparing for graduate school* means the program is *not for high school students.*
Choices (A) and (B) are explicitly mentioned. Choice (C) is not mentioned explicitly, but can be inferred.

195. (C) *Our instructors are seasoned by years of real-world business experience*, meaning *practical experience*.
Choices (A) and (B) are not mentioned. Choice (D) is contradicted by *there's only one accredited university recognized for its experience and excellence in on-line programs;* the program is already accredited.

196. (C) *Wherever you and your computer happen to be* means that one needs a computer to *commute to class by modem*.
Choices (A), (B), and (D) are not mentioned.

197. (A) The memo is from *James Carlson, Vice-President.*
Choices (B), (C), and (D) are contradicted by *From: James Carlson.*

198. (B) Artificial respiration is used in cases such as *smoke inhalation*, meaning *breathing too much smoke*.
Choices (A), (C), and (D) are not mentioned.

199. (C) *Clear mouth and throat of any obstruction with your fingers.*
Choices (A), (B), and (D) are contradicted by *with your fingers.*

200. (D) Employees are not told to *leave fingers in the patient's mouth to clear obstructions* while blowing into the patient's mouth.
Choices (A), (B), and (C) are explicitly mentioned.

TEST

two

TEST OF ENGLISH FOR INTERNATIONAL COMMUNICATION

General Directions

This is a test of your ability to use the English language. The total time for the test is approximately two and a half hours. It is divided into seven parts. Each part of the test begins with a set of specific directions. Be sure you understand what you are to do before you begin to work on a part.

You will find that some of the questions are harder than others, but you should try to answer every one. There is no penalty for guessing. Do not be concerned if you cannot answer all of the questions.

Do not mark your answers in this test book. **You must put all of your answers on the separate answer sheet** that you have been given. When putting your answer to a question on your answer sheet, be sure to fill in the answer space corresponding to the letter of your choice. Fill in the space so that the letter inside the oval cannot be seen, as shown in the example below.

EXAMPLE

Mr. Palmer _____ with the president last month.
(A)   meet
(B)   meeting
(C)   met
(D)   to meet

Sample Answer: (A)   (B)   ●   (D)

The sentence should read, "Mr. Palmer met with the president last month." Therefore, you should choose answer (C). Notice how this has been done in the example given.

Mark only **ONE** answer for each question. If you change your mind about an answer after you have marked it on your answer sheet, completely erase your old answer and then mark your new answer. You must mark the answer sheet carefully so that your score can be recorded accurately.

LISTENING COMPREHENSION

In this section of the test, you will have the chance to show how well you understand spoken English. There are four parts to this section, with special directions for each part.

Directions

For each question, you will see a picture in your test book and you will hear four short statements. The statements will be spoken just one time. They will not be written in your test book, so you must listen carefully to understand what the speaker says.

When you hear the four statements, look at the picture in your test book and choose the statement that best describes what you see in the picture. Then, on your answer sheet, find the number of the question and mark your answer. Look at the sample below.

EXAMPLE

Now listen to the four statements.

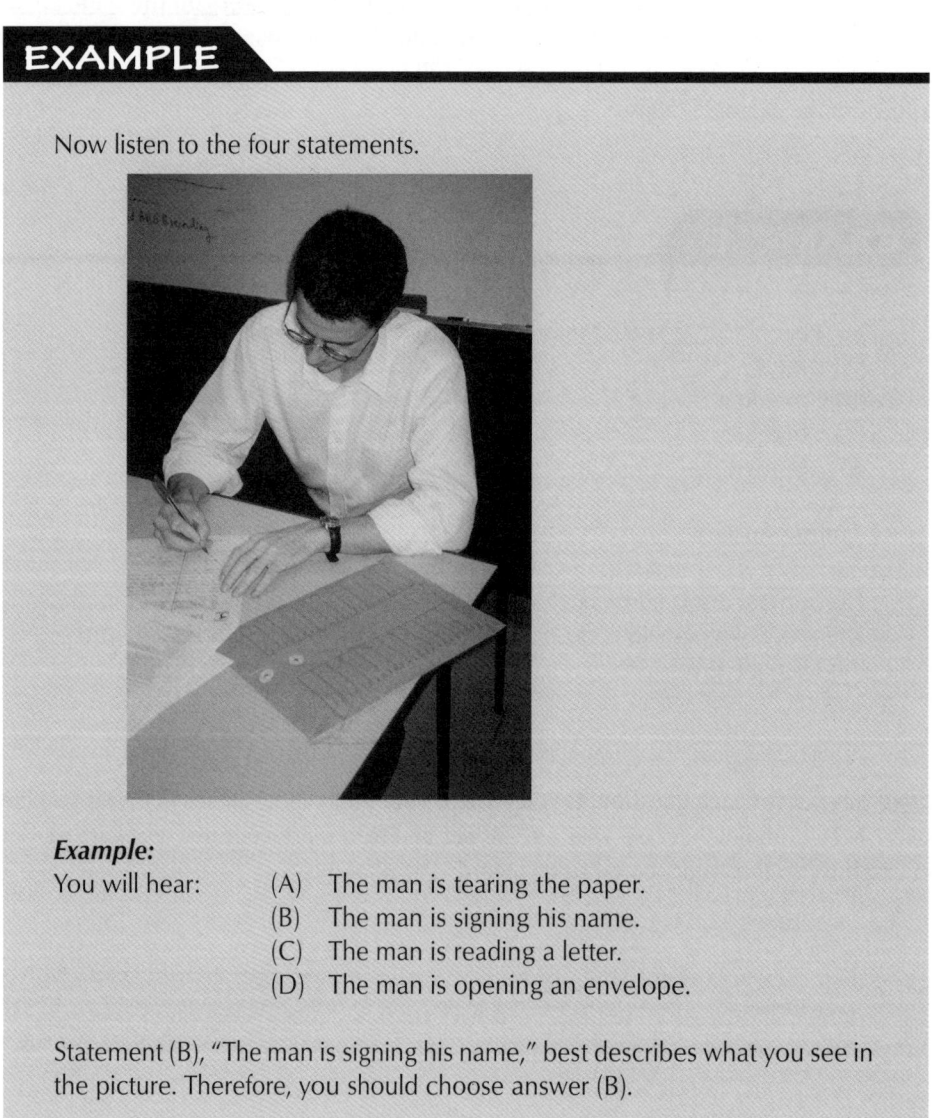

Example:

You will hear:
- (A) The man is tearing the paper.
- (B) The man is signing his name.
- (C) The man is reading a letter.
- (D) The man is opening an envelope.

Statement (B), "The man is signing his name," best describes what you see in the picture. Therefore, you should choose answer (B).

1

2

3

GO ON TO THE NEXT PAGE

7

8

9

GO ON TO THE NEXT PAGE

10

11

12

13

14

15

GO ON TO THE NEXT PAGE

16 ▶

17 ▶

18 ▶

19

20

GO ON TO THE NEXT PAGE

Directions

In this part of the test, you will hear a question spoken in English, followed by three responses, also spoken in English. The question and the responses will be spoken just one time. They will not be written out for you. You must listen carefully to understand what you hear. You are to choose the best response to each question.

EXAMPLE

Now listen to a sample question.

You will hear: Good morning, John. How are you?

You will also hear: (A) I am fine, thank you.
                   (B) I am in the living room.
                   (C) My name is John.

The best response to the question "How are you?" is choice (A), "I am fine, thank you." Therefore, you should choose answer (A).

21. Mark your answer on your answer sheet.
22. Mark your answer on your answer sheet.
23. Mark your answer on your answer sheet.
24. Mark your answer on your answer sheet.
25. Mark your answer on your answer sheet.
26. Mark your answer on your answer sheet.
27. Mark your answer on your answer sheet.
28. Mark your answer on your answer sheet.
29. Mark your answer on your answer sheet.
30. Mark your answer on your answer sheet.
31. Mark your answer on your answer sheet.
32. Mark your answer on your answer sheet.
33. Mark your answer on your answer sheet.
34. Mark your answer on your answer sheet.
35. Mark your answer on your answer sheet.

36. Mark your answer on your answer sheet.
37. Mark your answer on your answer sheet.
38. Mark your answer on your answer sheet.
39. Mark your answer on your answer sheet.
40. Mark your answer on your answer sheet.
41. Mark your answer on your answer sheet.
42. Mark your answer on your answer sheet.
43. Mark your answer on your answer sheet.
44. Mark your answer on your answer sheet.
45. Mark your answer on your answer sheet.
46. Mark your answer on your answer sheet.
47. Mark your answer on your answer sheet.
48. Mark your answer on your answer sheet.
49. Mark your answer on your answer sheet.
50. Mark your answer on your answer sheet.

Directions

In this part of the test, you will hear short conversations between two people. The conversations will not be written in your test book. You will hear the conversations only once; therefore, you must listen carefully.

In your test book, you will read a short question about each conversation. The question will be followed by four short answers. You are to choose the best answer to each question and mark it on your answer sheet.

51. What does the woman want from the man?
    (A) To change her lock
    (B) To travel to a conference
    (C) To water her plants
    (D) To exchange keys

52. What is Jack's problem?
    (A) He cannot find Ms. Williams.
    (B) He does not know which form to use.
    (C) He does not know who should sign the form.
    (D) He doesn't know if office expenses are reimbursable.

53. What is the man wondering?
    (A) How long the expressway will be rerouted
    (B) If the information about the expressway is correct
    (C) How long it would take to commute by subway
    (D) Where the subway station is

54. What happened to the woman's computer the day before?
    (A) It worked slowly.
    (B) It overheated.
    (C) It didn't work.
    (D) It lost addresses.

55. What does she suggest to Bill?
    (A) He should work on his budget.
    (B) He should go out to lunch.
    (C) She will bring him back lunch.
    (D) She will help him with the report.

56. What is Michael being asked to do?
    (A) Have another interview.
    (B) Resubmit a resume.
    (C) Ask Kathy Jones if she has his resume.
    (D) Check his printer.

57. What was Mrs. Yee's problem?
    (A) She didn't know about the stopover.
    (B) She missed her connection to Manila.
    (C) She didn't understand the directions in Hawaii.
    (D) She took the wrong flight.

58. What does the woman want to know?
    (A) Who else from the office is going to the wedding
    (B) What time they should leave
    (C) If she should drive to the party
    (D) If the man is going home before the party

GO ON TO THE NEXT PAGE

59. How has the appearance of the office changed?
- (A) The clocks were fixed.
- (B) There is a new computer screen.
- (C) The room is cleaner.
- (D) Everything was rearranged.

60. Where does this conversation take place?
- (A) At the dentist's
- (B) At the office
- (C) At City Center
- (D) At a birthday party

61. What is Mr. Palmer waiting for?
- (A) A shipment from Australia
- (B) The package from Zurich
- (C) Documents from New York
- (D) A delivery from Jakarta

62. What are they discussing?
- (A) Who will be working in August
- (B) Where Toby will go on vacation
- (C) When they took their vacation
- (D) How long it will take to fill back orders

63. What does the man want to know?
- (A) If the company has received a patent
- (B) If Gray and Kanter were hired
- (C) If the firm has found a consultant
- (D) If the search will be international

64. How many additional chairs will they need?
- (A) Six
- (B) Ten
- (C) Sixty-five
- (D) Seventy-five

65. Why is Joe asking about the Dynasty?
- (A) He needs to entertain visitors.
- (B) He is hungry.
- (C) He wants to know when it is open.
- (D) He wants to find a place near home.

66. What does the man inform Shell International?
- (A) The changes will not be made until next month.
- (B) Shell International can pay one amount for all changes.
- (C) The goods won't be ready until next month.
- (D) There will be a charge for each change made.

67. What do the decorators want to do?
- (A) Negotiate the sale price.
- (B) Finalize the paperwork.
- (C) Visit the office building.
- (D) Attend the closing.

68. What does the man suggest to Monica?
- (A) She should review the merger report.
- (B) She should read his book.
- (C) She should catch up on her sleep.
- (D) She should go on vacation.

69. What is the problem?
- (A) Mr. Jimenez is late for his meeting with Bill Carter.
- (B) Bill Carter is sorry that he is late for the appointment.
- (C) Mr. Jimenez needs another half hour with his client.
- (D) Bill Carter misunderstood when to meet Mr. Jimenez.

70. What are they discussing?
- (A) An accounting system
- (B) A computer problem
- (C) A broken TV screen
- (D) A language class

71. When does she suggest they see the exhibit?
- (A) September first
- (B) Anytime he is available
- (C) On a weekend
- (D) Wednesday evening

72. How does the man propose to promote the company?
    (A) By reprinting the brochures
    (B) By visiting prospective customers
    (C) By producing a video
    (D) By sending out materials this week

73. Where has Judy been?
    (A) Replacing Ann
    (B) Taking care of Ann
    (C) Home with the flu
    (D) Sitting upstairs

74. What time is the train?
    (A) At noon
    (B) At 1:00
    (C) At 3:00
    (D) At 4:00

75. Why did Panther Publishing consider buying Foster Mill?
    (A) Because of its location
    (B) Because of its size
    (C) The employees wanted to move.
    (D) They wanted to be downtown.

76. What is true about hotels built before 1985?
    (A) They will not need to have sprinkler systems.
    (B) The sprinkler systems were installed when the hotels were built.
    (C) They must install sprinkler systems by next year.
    (D) By this March they must install sprinkler systems.

77. What is Patty's occupation?
    (A) A fitness instructor
    (B) A cafeteria worker
    (C) An editor
    (D) An accountant

78. What does the man want to know?
    (A) How to get a merit raise
    (B) How often he'll get paid
    (C) How much he'll get paid
    (D) How to recommend his supervisor

79. Why is the woman upset?
    (A) She wanted to go with the man.
    (B) She did not know he would be away.
    (C) She did not know where he was going.
    (D) She wanted to send something with him.

80. What is the woman's job?
    (A) She's David's supervisor.
    (B) She's the export director.
    (C) She organizes trade fairs.
    (D) She's the vice-president for sales.

GO ON TO THE NEXT PAGE

Directions

In this part of the test, you will hear several short talks. Each will be spoken just one time. They will not be written out for you; therefore, you will have to listen carefully in order to understand and remember what is said.

In your test book, you will read two or more questions about each short talk. The questions will be followed by four answers. You are to choose the best answer to each question and mark it on your answer sheet.

81. Why is this announcement being made?
    (A) To explain the agenda items.
    (B) To notify families of the bus route.
    (C) To invite people to a picnic.
    (D) To announce new club hours.

82. What time will the event take place?
    (A) 11:30 a.m.
    (B) 12:00 p.m.
    (C) 1:00 p.m.
    (D) 4:00 p.m.

83. By when should people respond?
    (A) July 25
    (B) July 27
    (C) 11:30 sharp
    (D) The middle of the month

84. What was the purpose of the competition?
    (A) To select a company mascot.
    (B) To create a new product.
    (C) To distribute products.
    (D) To name the teddy bear.

85. About how many people entered the contest?
    (A) 25
    (B) 10,000
    (C) 17,000
    (D) 20,000

86. How will the winner be selected?
    (A) The name which gets the most votes.
    (B) The staff of ten will decide.
    (C) A name will be chosen in the cafeteria.
    (D) A lottery of the final twenty will be held.

87. What is being said about gold prices?
    (A) It is too early to report.
    (B) They are at a twenty-year low.
    (C) They are increasing.
    (D) They haven't been analyzed yet.

88. What is being advised?
    (A) To wait
    (B) To sell
    (C) To buy
    (D) To diversify

89. When should prices increase?
    (A) At the end of next year
    (B) By the first of the month
    (C) Before the new year
    (D) After the beginning of the new year

90. What is the main purpose of this announcement?
    (A) To report Ms. Forsyth's accident.
    (B) To notify the company of Ms. Forsyth's death.
    (C) To discuss Ms. Forsyth's floral preferences.
    (D) To review the route Ms. Forsyth traveled.

91. What caused the accident?
    (A) Bad weather
    (B) An airplane
    (C) Highway conditions
    (D) An animal

92. What is being advertised?
    (A) International communication
    (B) A cheap way to travel
    (C) Skydiving
    (D) A passport service

93. Who is making this advertisement?
    (A) A commerical airline
    (B) A medical facility
    (C) A travel agent
    (D) A courier service

94. How many flights are there weekly?
    (A) 21
    (B) 80
    (C) 700
    (D) 1,400

95. What is this announcement about?
    (A) Installing a telephone
    (B) Adding phone lines
    (C) New hiring procedures
    (D) Responding to customer inquiries

96. What will be different?
    (A) The number of employees
    (B) The hours of operation
    (C) The number of phone lines
    (D) The elimination of the busy signal

97. How many phone lines will be operational on Monday?
    (A) Ten
    (B) Fifteen
    (C) Twenty-five
    (D) Sixty

98. What is being discussed?
    (A) Far East ventures
    (B) Strip mining
    (C) Travel plans
    (D) A development project

99. Which of the following was NOT mentioned?
    (A) A hotel
    (B) A coastline marina
    (C) Shopping areas
    (D) Apartments

100. Why was Diamond, Black, and Epp selected?
    (A) Because of its relationship with the building commission
    (B) Because of its familiarity with this coastline
    (C) Because of its experience with similar projects
    (D) Because it is located in the Far East

This is the end of the Listening Comprehension portion of the test. Turn to Part V in your test book.

GO ON TO THE NEXT PAGE

READING

In this section of the test, you will have the chance to show how well you understand written English. There are three parts to this section, with special directions for each part.

Directions

This part of the test has incomplete sentences. Four words or phrases, marked (A), (B), (C), (D), are given beneath each sentence. You are to choose the **ONE** word or phrase that best completes the sentence. Then, on your answer sheet, find the number of the question and mark your answer.

EXAMPLE

Because the equipment is very delicate, it must be handled with _____ .
(A) caring
(B) careful
(C) care
(D) carefully

The sentence should read, "Because the equipment is very delicate, it must be handled with care." Therefore, you should choose answer (C).

Now begin work on the questions.

101. There were two finalists for the position, but _____ agreed to the salary offered.
(A) both
(B) all
(C) neither
(D) either

102. _____ the offer, the more pressure we'll have to accept.
(A) The greatest
(B) The greater
(C) More of
(D) Most of

103. In order to find the ratio, divide one number _____ the other.
(A) to
(B) in
(C) over
(D) by

104. Weren't you surprised that he cut his hair by _____?
(A) himself
(B) him
(C) hisself
(D) his

105. If it is _____, we will postpone the meeting until next week.
(A) accordingly
(B) accessorized
(C) acceptable
(D) accountable

106. The secretary _____ the travel agency make the arrangements.
(A) asked
(B) got
(C) had
(D) hired

107. The first _____ airmail service in the world started on May 15, 1918.
(A) continuous
(B) continuation
(C) continuity
(D) continuum

108. After touring the facility, the visitors ate lunch _____.
(A) arranged
(B) surrounding
(C) beside
(D) together

109. _____ the cost, a new identification system will be implemented next month.
(A) In spite
(B) Despite
(C) Although
(D) Nevertheless

110. The design department had two weeks to _____ a proposal.
(A) come by
(B) come over
(C) come up with
(D) come back

111. Each lane in the new fifty-kilometer highway is three and a half meters _____.
(A) wide
(B) width
(C) widely
(D) widen

112. There has not been a _____ in May since 1908.
(A) snowy
(B) snowstorm
(C) snowing
(D) storm of snow

113. The firm needs to employ two _____ since Mr. Yasuda and Miss Wing were transferred.
(A) accounting
(B) accounts
(C) accountants
(D) accounted

114. Automated teller machines enable people to do their banking at anytime, seven days _____.
(A) weekly
(B) week
(C) in a week
(D) a week

115. If the air conditioning should _____, call this number immediately.
(A) break down
(B) break up
(C) break into
(D) break through

116. The cause of the fire is still under _____.
(A) investigator
(B) investigating
(C) investigation
(D) investigate

GO ON TO THE NEXT PAGE

117. The engineer, _____ desk you will be using this month, is on vacation.
- (A) who
- (B) whose
- (C) which
- (D) with a

118. Although the shippers are twins, they seem nothing _____.
- (A) unlike
- (B) likely
- (C) like
- (D) alike

119. _____, he was not considered for the job.
- (A) Due to his lack of experience
- (B) His lack of experience due to
- (C) Due to his experience a lack of
- (D) His experience lack of due to

120. Customer satisfaction is at an _____ high.
- (A) very
- (B) ever-increasingly
- (C) all-time
- (D) especially

121. The banking system in most countries consists of several large banks with many branches _____.
- (A) nationalize
- (B) national
- (C) nationality
- (D) nationwide

122. In some corporations, employees _____ offices, desks, and room assignments.
- (A) circle
- (B) rotate
- (C) take turns
- (D) exercise

123. Michigan is _____ to Minnesota in iron ore production.
- (A) second only
- (B) among second
- (C) only
- (D) by second

124. The marketing department, which had argued for investing, decided _____ to wait and see.
- (A) secondly
- (B) at second best
- (C) on second hand
- (D) on second thought

125. There are regulations governing the amount of sleep _____ must get in a twenty-four hour span.
- (A) flight's attendants
- (B) flights attendants
- (C) flight attendants
- (D) a flight's attendant

126. The finance committee should _____ its recommendation to the public on Friday.
- (A) have been made
- (B) be made
- (C) made
- (D) have made

127. Payments can be made monthly or _____ month.
- (A) each
- (B) another
- (C) every other
- (D) one another

128. The resort encourages visitors to _____ the brochure before making a reservation.
- (A) look through
- (B) look around
- (C) look forward to
- (D) look up to

129. _____, workers at Digitech Corporation spend five hours a day in front of a computer screen.
   (A) It is averaged
   (B) On the average
   (C) The average that
   (D) The average

130. Many buyers complained that the new model was _____ to the old one.
   (A) worse
   (B) lower
   (C) beneath
   (D) inferior

131. Juan was delighted to hear of _____ opening in the Lisbon office.
   (A) another
   (B) other
   (C) the others
   (D) other ones

132. Please join us in bidding a fond _____ to Mrs. Okada at a celebration on Saturday.
   (A) expression
   (B) farewell
   (C) party
   (D) ceremony

133. The pamphlets will have to _____ before they can be packaged for mailing.
   (A) alphabetize
   (B) be alphabetized
   (C) be alphabetizing
   (D) alphabetical

134. The agents who had the highest gross _____ last month were recognized at the banquet.
   (A) indexes
   (B) money
   (C) profits
   (D) national product

135. Before you leave for the airport, call the airline to make sure your flight is _____.
   (A) at time
   (B) by time
   (C) in time
   (D) on time

136. The recently-hired secretary is an old friend of _____.
   (A) my
   (B) mine
   (C) me
   (D) myself

137. Before you are considered for your next promotion, I will _____ for you.
   (A) put a word in good
   (B) in a good word put
   (C) a good word put in
   (D) put in a good word

138. The company physician recommended that Paul _____ more exercise.
   (A) get
   (B) gets
   (C) is getting
   (D) will get

139. _____ it took Mrs. Roth one month to calculate what she can now do in one day.
   (A) Before ten years
   (B) Ten years ago
   (C) Ten years past
   (D) Before ten years ago

140. The price at the downtown hotel is the same for single or double _____.
   (A) payment
   (B) tenant
   (C) occupancy
   (D) possession

GO ON TO THE NEXT PAGE

Directions

In this part of the test, each sentence has four words or phrases underlined. The four underlined parts of the sentence are marked (A), (B), (C), (D). You are to identify the **ONE** underlined word or phrase that should be corrected or rewritten. Then, on your answer sheet, find the number of the question and mark your answer.

EXAMPLE

All <u>employee</u> are required <u>to wear</u> their <u>identification</u> badges <u>while</u> at work.
　　A　　　　　　　　　　B　　　　　　C　　　　　　　　D

Choice (A), the underlined word "employee," is not correct in this sentence. The sentence should read, "All employees are required to wear their identification badges while at work." Therefore, you should choose answer (A).

Now begin work on the questions.

141. Diamond Carpets <u>has used</u> both print
　　　　　　　　　　A
advertisements <u>or</u> radio announcements to
　　　　　　　　B
<u>announce</u> the <u>end-of-the-year</u> sale.
　　C　　　　　　　D

142. <u>As a result</u> of the changes <u>made</u> in 1977 and
　　　A　　　　　　　　　　　　B
1983, social security revenue <u>begun</u> to
　　　　　　　　　　　　　　　　C
increase <u>significantly</u> in 1988.
　　　　　　D

143. Tattooing is done by pricking <u>small</u> holes in
　　　　　　　　　　　　　　　A
the skin with a <u>sharpened</u> stick, bone, or
　　　　　　　　B
needle that <u>has dipped</u> in pigments with
　　　　　　　C
<u>natural</u> colors.
　　D

144. Tangelo is <u>a</u> mandarin citrus fruit <u>that</u> results
　　　　　　A　　　　　　　　　　　B
from cross pollination <u>among</u> a tangerine
　　　　　　　　　　　C
<u>and</u> a grapefruit.
　D

145. <u>Not one</u> should order <u>merchandise</u> <u>on</u> the
　　A　　　　　　　B　　　　C
telephone with an <u>unknown</u> company.
　　　　　　　　D

146. For many years, Akron was <u>by far</u> the
　　　　　　　　　　　　　　A
world's <u>most largest</u> manufacturer of tires,
　　　　　B
<u>and</u> its factories produced a variety of <u>other</u>
　C　　　　　　　　　　　　　　　D
items.

147. Unlike most natural fibers, manufactured
     A   B
     fibers are produced in long, continuation
              C   D
     lengths, called filaments.

148. Tape recordings can easy be edited by
                          A   B
     cutting out the unwanted sections and then
                                        C
     joining the ends of the tape together.
            D

149. Quartz-based watches appeared in the early
                                          A
     1970's, and because their accuracy soon
                    B   C
     made earlier electric watches obsolete.
          D

150. Every shipment entering the United States is
     A   B
     subject to more than five hundred pages of
     C
     customs and tariff regulation.
                          D

151. Once the warehouse is total computerized,
     A   B
     customers will receive their shipments
        C
     in half the time they do now.
        D

152. Blue Star International announced yesterday

     that Mr. Lucas Jones he will be promoted to
                          A   B
     Director of Exports effective immediately.
                          C   D

153. Because the company had advertised the
     A   B
     position in a local newspaper, the number of

     inquiries was surprising and unexpected.
              C   D

154. Living abroad requires knowledge of a
                    A
     country's language, business customs, and the
     B   C
     social, economics, and political institutions.
            D

155. The company finally decided to buy the
                  A   B
     more expensive computers because they are
                               C
     more easier to use.
     D

156. A poll revealed that consumer preference for
            A
     a product raises by 19 percent after its
               B   C   D
     appearance on a small airship or blimp.

157. The company was surprised that so many
                                   A   B
     employees did not seem to be doing progress
                       C   D
     with the new computer system.

158. In some countries, exchanging business

     cards at a first meeting is considering a basic
             A B   C
     part of good business etiquette.
             D

159. If you wish to attend any session at the
                 A   B
     symposium next week, you should inform
                                C
     the personnel director toward Friday.
                            D

160. Rates for domestic air service are now based
                                    A
     on the distance a letter or package is sent

     in addition to its weigh.
     B   C   D

GO ON TO THE NEXT PAGE

Directions

The questions in this part of the test are based on a variety of reading material, such as notices, letters, newspapers and magazine articles, and advertisements. You are to choose the **ONE** best answer, (A), (B), (C), or (D), to each question. Then, on your answer sheet, find the number of the question and mark your answer. Answer all questions following a passage on the basis of what is **stated** or **implied** in that passage.

EXAMPLE

Read the following example.

> The Museum of Technology is designed for people to experience science at work. Visitors are encouraged to use, test, and handle the objects on display. Special demonstrations are scheduled for the first and second Wednesdays of each month at 1:30 p.m. Open Tuesday-Friday, 2:30-4:30 p.m., Saturday 11:00 a.m.-4:30 p.m., and Sunday 1:00-4:30 p.m.

When during the month can visitors see special demonstrations?
(A)   Every weekend
(B)   The first two Wednesdays
(C)   One afternoon a week
(D)   Every other Wednesday

The passage says that the demonstrations are scheduled on the first and second Wednesdays of the month. Therefore, you should choose answer (B).

Now begin work on the questions.

Questions 161–163 refer to the following advertisement.

MBA INFORMATION SESSIONS
Learn the value of customizing your degree

The Bentwood MBA now has eight concentrations:
- Accounting
- Environmental Management
- International Business
- Operations Management
- Business Economics
- Finance
- Marketing

Advanced standing credit and one-week courses may reduce the amount of time needed to complete Bentwood's nationally recognized program.

Learn how Bentwood can make your MBA more relevant to your career interests at the August 12th Information Session at 6:30 p.m.

For more information or to reserve your spot, call or e-mail us.

161. Someone planning to work in which field would apply to Bentwood?
(A) Custom tailoring
(B) Marketing
(C) Architecture
(D) Law

162. How can someone reduce the amount of time needed to complete the program?
(A) By taking only one-week courses
(B) By working at the same time
(C) By transferring credits
(D) By taking more courses in one term

163. How should someone contact Bentwood?
(A) By telephone
(B) By faxing
(C) By filling out a form
(D) In a letter

Questions 164–167 refer to the following advertisement.

AGENTS/DISTRIBUTORS

Leading Australian manufacturer of pure New World quilts, comforter sets, and pillows, currrently exporting to Asia and Europe, would like to expand its international contacts to include the U.S.A.

We are looking for Agents/Distributors with experience selling products within the bedding industry. A representative of the company will be visiting the United States at the end of July.

For information and appointments, please contact us by fax at 613-977-8900.

Send us your salary requirements, a resume, and names and addresses of three references.

---

164. Where might this company currently do business?
- (A) New York
- (B) Mexico City
- (C) Montreal
- (D) Seoul

165. What product does this company produce?
- (A) Napkins
- (B) Bed frames
- (C) Sheets
- (D) Towels

166. Where will an interview take place?
- (A) In Australia
- (B) In the U.S.
- (C) In Europe
- (D) In Asia

167. What information should an interested candidate supply?
- (A) Desired wages
- (B) Age
- (C) Earned degrees
- (D) Languages spoken

Questions 168–170 refer to the following news article.

On Friday the Brazilian stock market was flat in slow trading as investors stayed on the sidelines waiting for large players to make their next moves to push shares up. Equities edged up as cash-rich domestic pension-fund managers bought up telecommunications and banking stocks, continuing the previous day's upward trend.

168. What happened to Brazilian stocks on Friday?
(A) They continued their upward trend.
(B) They edged up dramatically.
(C) They remained unchanged.
(D) They were traded.

169. What are stock investors waiting for?
(A) A move in banking stocks
(B) Purchases by larger investors
(C) A rise in telecommunication stocks
(D) Loans from pension-fund managers

170. Why are pension-fund managers investing?
(A) They are looking for international investments.
(B) They are following the upward trend.
(C) They want to help out small players.
(D) They have a lot of cash to invest.

GO ON TO THE NEXT PAGE

Questions 171–174 refer to the following advertisement.

WINDBORN CRUISES

180 degrees from the ordinary

Windborn's sleek 440-foot cruise ships
offer an extraordinary way to explore Tahiti,
the Caribbean, and the Mediterranean.
On board are 74 luxurious cabins,
each facing the sea.
A staff of 88, and 6 spectacular dining rooms.
Take a 12-, 14-, or 21-day cruise.
Enjoy swimming, tennis, and aerobics classes.
Nightly entertainment.

Call for our free brochure. Norwegian registry.

171. What can travelers do on board?
(A) Swim
(B) Play badminton
(C) Use a treadmill
(D) Scuba dive

172. What do the cabins face?
(A) The classes
(B) The dining rooms
(C) The sea
(D) The entertainment

173. How many people work on the ship?
(A) 74
(B) 88
(C) 140
(D) 440

174. What is the maximum number of weeks for one cruise?
(A) One
(B) Two
(C) Three
(D) Four

Questions 175–177 refer to the following bulletin.

When "**Picasso: The Early Years, 1892-1906**" opens at the Museum of Fine Arts on September 15, it will not only delight visitors with well-known examples of Pablo Picasso's work from his Blue and Rose Periods — it will also intrigue and surprise visitors with other less familiar, but equally astonishing drawings, paintings, and sculptures. Because of the large turnout anticipated for this special two-month exhibition, each ticket will be issued for a specific date and half-hour of entry. Tickets go on sale to the general public at $15 per person on July 15.

175. What kinds of works will be exhibited?
(A) Photographs
(B) Floral arrangements
(C) Weavings
(D) Sculptures

176. What is true about the exhibit?
(A) Tickets do not specify a time of entry.
(B) Visitors can buy a ticket and see the exhibit on July 15.
(C) Picasso's works from his Blue and Red Periods are well known.
(D) Picasso's works from before 1906 are not well known.

177. When will the exhibit close?
(A) July
(B) September
(C) October
(D) November

GO ON TO THE NEXT PAGE

HEALTH INSURANCE CHANGES

Effective with the calendar
year of 1999, every new employee must
choose Pilgrim Health Plan
as their medical insurer.

Those employees currently on
the Bay State or Federal Plans may
remain with those carriers.
Current employees wishing to change
insurers may select only Pilgrim.
Single employees will pay 10% of the
costs, and those choosing the family
plan will pay 25%.
Dental coverage will be available at no
additional cost only with the Pilgrim Plan.

178. What does this announcement define?
(A) Wage scales
(B) Health benefits
(C) Tax laws
(D) Dental plans

179. If the cost of a health plan for one year were $2,000, how much would a single employee contribute?
(A) $20
(B) $100
(C) $200
(D) $250

180. To whom is this paragraph generally addressed?
(A) Doctors and dentists
(B) Single employees
(C) Medical insurers
(D) Company workers

181. If an employee is hired on February 6, 1999, which plan must he choose?
(A) Pilgrim
(B) Bay State
(C) Federal
(D) Whichever he wants

The B.A. Beagle Company
announced higher-than-
expected profits for the
second quarter ending July 31.
The announcement caused
the stock to rise to
a 52-week high of 32 1/8.
Analysts attributed the
increased profits to cost-
cutting measures which were
implemented after the arrival
of President A. J. Donaldson in
January of last year.

182. When was this announcement made?
(A) In the first quarter
(B) During the second quarter
(C) On July 31 of last year
(D) After July 31 of this year

183. What reason did analysts give for the rise in
the stock price?
(A) Better pricing conditions
(B) Reduction in expenses
(C) Decrease in productivity
(D) A rising stock market

184. How long has the president been with the
company?
(A) Since July 31
(B) Less than ten months
(C) At least a year
(D) Fifty-two weeks

GO ON TO THE NEXT PAGE

Questions 185–188 refer to the following bulletin.

The highway department announced today the closing of two of the four lanes in each direction on Highway 635. The lanes will be closed for six to eight months for repair work.

This will include repaving, installation of new guard rails, and improved lighting. The speed limit will be reduced to 35 miles per hour, which will be strictly enforced by the police.

Exit 40 will be closed for the duration of construction. Traffic to Route 135 will use Exit 41.

Electronic message boards will update traffic conditions.

185. What is the subject of the announcement?
    (A) Highway repairs
    (B) A new highway
    (C) Increased speed limits
    (D) New toll booths

186. How many total lanes will the highway have when work is complete?
    (A) Two
    (B) Four
    (C) Eight
    (D) Sixteen

187. How will the speed limit be monitored?
    (A) By electronic message boards
    (B) By the highway department
    (C) By new guard rails
    (D) By the police

188. What should drivers who want to exit to Route 135 do?
    (A) Take Exit 40.
    (B) Stay on the highway.
    (C) Take a different exit.
    (D) Observe the speed limit.

WINSTON PUBLISHERS, INTERNATIONAL

THIS AGREEMENT BETWEEN _____ AND WINSTON PUBLISHERS, INTERNATIONAL IS GOVERNED IN ACCORDANCE WITH THE LAWS OF THE REPUBLIC OF SINGAPORE, REGARDLESS OF THE PLACE OF THE PHYSICAL EXECUTION OF AGREEMENT.

THIS AGREEMENT IS MADE THIS _____ DAY OF _____, 19___, BETWEEN WINSTON PUBLISHERS AND _____, HEREINAFTER CALLED AUTHOR.

1. THE PUBLISHER HAS THE RIGHT TO PUBLISH AND DISTRIBUTE THE WORK IN ANY LANGUAGE THROUGHOUT THE WORLD.

2. THE AUTHOR VERIFIES THAT THE WORK IS ORIGINAL, EXCEPT FOR EXCERPTS FROM COPYRIGHTED WORKS INCLUDED WITH PROPER PERMISSION.

3. THE AUTHOR AGREES TO DELIVER TO PUBLISHER ON OR BEFORE THE _____ DAY OF _____, 19___, TWO DOUBLE-SPACED WORD-PROCESSED COPIES AND CORRESPONDING DISCS INCLUDING ALL PHOTOGRAPHS, DRAWINGS, DIAGRAMS, TABLES, AND SUPPLEMENTARY INSTRUCTIONAL MATERIAL, IF REQUIRED BY THE PUBLISHER.

4. THE PUBLISHER AGREES TO PAY AUTHOR ROYALTIES OF 10% BASED ON NET AMOUNT RECEIVED BY THE PUBLISHER FOR EACH COPY SOLD IN ASIA, EXCLUDING SALES TAXES, TRANSPORTATION CHARGES, AND RETURNS.

5. THE PUBLISHER AGREES TO GIVE AUTHOR SIX FREE COPIES OF THE WORK AND TO SELL COPIES TO THE AUTHOR AT A DISCOUNT OF 40% OFF LIST PRICE.

189. Under which country's jurisdiction does this contract operate?
(A) The country where the author resides
(B) The country where the contract was signed
(C) The country of Singapore
(D) The country where a dispute occurs

190. What must be original?
(A) The entire work
(B) Everything except excerpts included with permission
(C) Translated works
(D) All photographs, drawings, and diagrams

191. What must the author supply?
(A) Proof of citizenship
(B) Two handwritten copies
(C) Copies of transportation charges
(D) Instructional material if requested

192. On what is the royalty calculated?
(A) Asian sales
(B) Worldwide sales
(C) The author's purchases
(D) Returned sales

GO ON TO THE NEXT PAGE

Questions 193–194 refer to the following brochure.

The exclusive 100-suite Carmel Valley Ranch in Monterey County, California, is offering three distinct packages that challenge every level of golfer.

For beginners or those who'd like to work on their game, a three-night **Instruction** package includes three hours of daily instruction, green fees and club rental. The three-night **Eagle** package includes two days of golf and cart rental. The five-night **Hole-in-One** package includes four Monterey Peninsula courses.

Summertime rates at the Carefree Resorts property range from $929 for a single golfer to $3,068 for a double, depending on the program selected.

193. Which package would be best for a novice golfer?
(A) The Instruction package
(B) The Eagle package
(C) The Hole-in-One package
(D) They are all equally suited.

194. Which of the following is true about the packages?
(A) They all cost the same.
(B) They all include cart rental.
(C) They are all at least three nights.
(D) They all include club rental.

Each summer Richard Bennett, a Cleveland clothier, offers customers $25 off a new, tailor-made suit for each old suit brought in. This promotion has worked so well that sales during the normally slack summer months of July and August almost match sales during May and June, traditionally the peak months for the sale of suits. His newspaper advertisement reads:

Charity Begins at Home
Retire your tired suits

Look into your closet and bring us those "I'll wear it when it rains" suits and get $25.00 off a new suit or sports coat-and-slacks combination for each old suit you bring in.
Your tired suit will be donated to the charity of your choice.
This charitable offer must end June 28th, so don't wait for a rainy day to see our exciting fall collections.

195. Why is the promotion in the summer?
(A) To make up for slow sales
(B) To take advantage of the rainy season
(C) To highlight the fall collections
(D) To assist retired customers

196. When are Richard Bennett's sales usually highest?
(A) During July and August
(B) During May and June
(C) On June 28
(D) In the fall

197. What happens to customers' old suits?
(A) A tailor makes them into new suits.
(B) They are sold to other customers.
(C) They are donated to charity.
(D) They are worn in the rain.

GO ON TO THE NEXT PAGE

Questions 198–200 refer to the following explanation.

Microcomputers are commonly known as personal computers (PCs); they usually fit on a desktop and some can even be held on one's lap — hence the terms *desktop* and *laptop* computers. Although micro-computers are the least powerful of the three types of computers, they still are more powerful than the first generation of computers. Microcomputers are popular with small businesses because they are relatively inexpensive, and thus within the financial reach of virtually every entrepreneur.

198. Where did the name *desktop* originate?
- (A) This term shows that these computers are inexpensive.
- (B) This term differentiates these computers from laptops.
- (C) These computers can only be used on a desktop.
- (D) These computers can fit on the top of a desk.

199. What can be said about the first generation of computers?
- (A) They are more powerful than laptop computers.
- (B) They are less powerful than all existing computers.
- (C) Their power diminished over time.
- (D) They became popular on desktops.

200. Why are PCs popular with small businesses?
- (A) Because they can be found everywhere.
- (B) Because they don't take up much office space.
- (C) Because they are so powerful.
- (D) Because they are not so expensive.

Stop! This is the end of the test. If you finish before time is called, you can go back to Parts V, VI, and VII and check your work.

TAPESCRIPT

Sample Item

M: (A) The man is tearing the paper.
(B) The man is signing his name.
(C) The man is reading a letter.
(D) The man is opening an envelope.

1. *F:* (A) The traffic light is over the direction signs.
(B) Pedestrians are crossing the street.
(C) Cars are blocking the crosswalk.
(D) Pedestrians are waiting for the light to change.

2. *M1:* (A) The customers are sitting on benches.
(B) The food is served only inside the restaurant.
(C) People are eating outside the restaurant.
(D) The restaurant is closed for the summer.

3. *M2:* (A) The man is about to kick the ball across the field.
(B) The man has tripped on the ball and fallen to the ground.
(C) The man is getting ready to tackle a member of the other team.
(D) The ball is about to hit the ground in front of the man.

4. *F:* (A) The police officer is holding back a crowd of people.
(B) The police officer is putting on a pair of sunglasses.
(C) The police officer is saluting in front of the crowd.
(D) The police officer's eyes aren't visible.

5. *M1:* (A) A man and woman are shaking hands.
(B) The two men are shaking hands.
(C) The woman is introducing her daughter to the men.
(D) The men are greeting one another.

6. *M2:* (A) The men are looking for a job.
(B) All the waiters are wearing bow ties.
(C) The three waiters are clearing the tables.
(D) One waiter has taken off his bow tie.

7. *F:* (A) The skiers' masks are covering their faces.
(B) The skiers are putting on their skis.
(C) The skiers are checking into the lodge.
(D) The skiers are waiting in line.

8. *M2:* (A) The factory produces a lot of smoke.
(B) There are many clouds in the sky.
(C) The factory is closed for repairs.
(D) The smokers are not allowed inside the factory.

9. *M1:* (A) The girl went out to purchase supplies for the class.
(B) The girl forgot to bring her materials to study outside.
(C) The girl is sitting outside on a bench studying.
(D) The girl is placing a bench against the brick wall.

10. *F:* (A) The building is being demolished.
(B) The men are painting the building's exterior.
(C) The painters are painting the inside of the building.
(D) The men are standing on ladders.

11. *M2:* (A) The girls are climbing a tree.
(B) The store is completely out of ice cream.
(C) The girls are sharing ice cream with their friends.
(D) The two girls are eating ice cream in a park.

12. *M1:* (A) The hotel is advertising its grand opening.
(B) The doorman is flagging down a taxi in front of the hotel.
(C) The flags are flying next to the main entrance.
(D) There are flags flying above the hotel sign.

13. *F:* (A) A group of people are crossing the street.
(B) Many people are waiting for the light to change.
(C) The people are trying to avoid the oncoming cars.
(D) The pedestrians have stopped at the "Don't Walk" sign.

14. *M1:* (A) The bull is running away from the bullfighter.
(B) The bullfighter is holding a cloth in front of the bull.
(C) The bullfighter is kneeling in front of the bull.
(D) The bull is entering the ring.

15. *M2:* (A) The man in the glasses has finished his performance.
(B) The spectators are amused.
(C) People in the crowd are clapping.
(D) The play has been canceled for today.

16. *F:* (A) Some people have already gotten their bags at the airport.
(B) The luggage has been stowed properly on the plane.
(C) All of the passengers are still waiting for their luggage to arrive.
(D) The baggage carousel is not operating.

17. *M2:* (A) The hotel clerk is lifting the keyboard onto the desk.
(B) The hotel clerk is making change for a guest.
(C) The hotel clerk is checking a reservation on the computer.
(D) The hotel clerk is handing over the room keys.

18. *M1:* (A) The woman is filling the dishwasher.
(B) The man and woman are setting the table.
(C) The couple is washing the dishes.
(D) The man and woman are cooking dinner.

19. *F:* (A) Lunch is being served by the waiters.
(B) The woman is paying for her lunch in the cafeteria.
(C) The woman is looking at the lunch menu.
(D) The woman is waiting for her food to arrive.

20. *M2:* (A) The referee is blowing the whistle.
(B) The referee is putting the whistle in his mouth.
(C) The referee is holding the whistle.
(D) The referee is talking to the players.

Sample Question

W: *Good morning, John. How are you?*

M: (A) I am fine, thank you.
M: (B) I am in the living room.
M: (C) My name is John.

21. *W:*   *Did you finish the report, Carlos?*
M: (A) I'm a reporter.
M: (B) Until tomorrow.
M: (C) I left it on your desk.

22. *M:*   *Have you seen my passport?*
W: (A) I got it in Spain.
W: (B) In the hotel room.
W: (C) To the airport.

23. *W:*   *Why weren't you at Joseph's going-away party?*
M: (A) I had to do the books.
M: (B) When I saw him last.
M: (C) I like parties a lot.

24. *M:*   *Do you have a typist?*
W: (A) Yes, I'll have some.
W: (B) No, I already have one.
W: (C) No, I do everything myself.

25. *W:*   *How long have you lived in this country?*
M: (A) Sometime next year.
M: (B) Six months.
M: (C) In the 1980s.

26. *M:*   *You got the promotion, didn't you?*
W: (A) I'm the new marketing director.
W: (B) I'll see you tomorrow.
W: (C) No, we need new computers.

27. *M:*   *Who's responsible for ordering the software?*
W: (A) It's in the wastebasket.
W: (B) Thank you. I'd like more information.
W: (C) That's Mr. Chan's job.

28. *W:*   *Should we leave tomorrow at 7:00 or at 8:00?*
M: (A) I'd prefer to eat at home.
M: (B) If it's OK with you, I'd rather leave later.
M: (C) I left at 8:00.

29. *M:*   *Weren't you surprised that he spoke for so long?*
W: (A) He doesn't speak Spanish.
W: (B) No, I didn't.
W: (C) I didn't know he had so much to say.

30. *W:*   *Would it be all right if I don't wear a tie?*
M: (A) As long as you wear a suit.
M: (B) I'll be tied up tomorrow.
M: (C) I don't like the blue tie.

31. *M:*   *How did you manage to take a two-week vacation?*
W: (A) You're right. I'm the new manager.
W: (B) I traded weeks with Steven.
W: (C) The resort was on the ocean.

32. *W:*   *So when are you filling the opening?*
M: (A) I hope next week.
M: (B) I'm feeling better.
M: (C) I'll close the window.

33. *M:*   *Would you mind if I watch you operate the new copy machine?*
W: (A) My fax machine makes copies.
W: (B) My watch is broken.
W: (C) No, go right ahead.

34. *M:*   *What's the sales quota for this month?*
W: (A) Yes, that's right.
W: (B) The same as last month.
W: (C) I've been there twice.

35. *W:*   *Do you think Mrs. Suzuki has signed up for the in-service training?*
M: (A) In the summer.
M: (B) The train has hourly service to the capital.
M: (C) I know she's planning to.

36. *M:*   *Is the lawyer going to meet with us here, or at his office?*
W: (A) I thought he said he'd let us know.
W: (B) No, but he will by Friday.
W: (C) It's on the fifteenth floor.

37. *M:*   *Does anyone know what happened to all the coffee cups?*
W: (A) Coffee stays warmer in china cups.
W: (B) About a hundred.
W: (C) We've all been asked to bring in our own reusable cups.

38. *W:*   *Why weren't you at the department meeting?*
M: (A) Every Friday at one.
M: (B) I thought it had been postponed.
M: (C) I'll be there.

39. *M:*   *Are you looking for a two- or four-door car?*
W: (A) Actually, what's more important is the price.
W: (B) I have two cars.
W: (C) Is it the blue one?

40. *W:*   *How soon can you have the documents translated?*
M: (A) Until Thursday, probably.
M: (B) Not before the first of the month.
M: (C) For a few weeks.

41. *M:*   *Mr. Young is on another line. May I take a message?*
W: (A) I can't wait for him.
W: (B) I've already taken one.
W: (C) I need to speak to him.

42. *W:*   *What did you think of the proposal?*
M: (A) No, I don't think so.
M: (B) I've been engaged since May.
M: (C) I haven't had a minute to look it over.

43. *M:*   *Are you the new employee on the fifth floor?*
W: (A) No, I work on the eighth.
W: (B) Yes, I'm leaving on the fifth.
W: (C) Yes, I have one.

44. W: *Who covers sales for Seoul?*
M: (A) The Korean reports are in the office.
M: (B) No, they're not.
M: (C) I think it's Peter Newport, but you'd better check.

45. M: *How much will our product be discounted?*
W: (A) 3,200 of them, not including present orders.
W: (B) They aren't very expensive.
W: (C) By twenty-five percent.

46. W: *Will you proofread my memo for me?*
M: (A) Sure, go ahead.
M: (B) I'm not too good with punctuation.
M: (C) I didn't read the memo.

47. M: *Where did you get your briefcase?*
W: (A) At the duty-free shop at the airport.
W: (B) It's not very long.
W: (C) It's leather, not vinyl.

48. W: *Have you sent out resumes to other companies?*
M: (A) No, I wasn't.
M: (B) Yes, I resume on Monday.
M: (C) No, I'm happy working here.

49. M: *Should I take a cab or go by bus to the airport?*
W: (A) Yes, you can.
W: (B) A taxi is quicker but more expensive.
W: (C) Well, I don't think that's a very good idea.

50. W: *Where did you learn to speak German?*
M: (A) In high school.
M: (B) For two years.
M: (C) It's a difficult language.

51. W: Do you think you could stop by my apartment and water my plants for me on Friday while I'm at the conference next week?
M: No problem. I still have your key you gave me last year.
W: Let me see it — I had the locks changed a few months ago.

52. M: Do you know what form I'm supposed to use to be reimbursed for office expenses?
W: I'm not sure which form it is, Jack, but it has to be signed by Ms. Williams.
M: Oh, then I'll ask her about it.

53. M: I just heard someone say the expressway is being rerouted for the next two weeks.
W: As if it wasn't bad enough before.
M: Have you ever taken the subway to work?

54. W: Have you heard the weather report for today?
M: If it's as hot as yesterday, I'm afraid my computer will barely work.
W: Yesterday, mine took an hour to pull up the addresses I needed.

55. W: Bill, are you eating here or going out for lunch?
M: I haven't decided, but I'll probably stay here and work on the budget report.
W: Tell me what you'd like and I'll bring it back for you.

56. W: Michael, the personnel office doesn't have a copy of your resume. Did you submit one at your interview?
M: I remember bringing it with me. But it's no problem to print another one.
W: Thanks. Make sure Kathy Jones has it by the end of the week.

57. M: Mrs. Yee, how was your flight to Manila?
W: Terrible. I was told it would be direct from Los Angeles, but there was a four-hour stopover in Hawaii.
M: Oh, no. That happened to me last time, too.

58. W: Were you invited to Sarah's engagement party?
M: I was afraid to ask you. Actually, I think we're the only ones from Scitech going.
W: Will you be going straight from work?

59. M: Have you noticed how much cleaner everything looks around here?
W: It must be the new service that started on Monday.
M: It was about time. The dust was so thick on my computer screen I couldn't see through it.

60. W: Can you recommend a good dentist? My tooth is killing me and I've asked everyone else in the office.
M: Do you remember meeting my cousin Brian? He's in practice down at the City Center.
W: He's a dentist? He looks seventeen.

61. M: You'll have to sign for these packages.
W: Oh, is it the documents from Jakarta? Mr. Palmer has been waiting for this.
M: Let's see. One's from New York. Another is from Zurich, and the last one's from Australia.

62. W: Christine, did you hear that we'll be closed the first week in August?
M: Oh yeah? No one told me.
W: Actually no one will be in the office, but the shipping department will be working, filling back orders.

63. M: Is the company still looking for a legal consultant?
W: I know they need someone with international patent expertise.
M: My last firm used Gray and Kanter. They were excellent.

64. W: How many people are we expecting for the seminar?
M: I think seventy-five. Let's borrow some chairs from the sixth-floor conference room.
W: Then we'll only need about ten — I think we can get them ourselves.

65. M: Have you tried the Sunday brunch at the Dynasty?
     W: Joe, I stay away from all-you-can-eat places. I always stuff myself.
     M: I thought it might be a good place to take the consultants from the home office.

66. W: Is this the Letter of Credit department? This is Shell International; I need to make an amendment.
     M: There'll be an additional charge for each change made.
     W: We have no choice. The goods won't be ready until next month.

67. M: When will we be closing the deal for the office building downtown?
     W: The paperwork is being finalized as we speak.
     M: Good, because I need to know when to tell the decorators they can see it.

68. M: Monica, I've got a great book for you to take on your trip.
     W: Are you kidding? When I'm not sleeping, I'll be reviewing the three-hundred-page merger report.
     M: Take it anyway. It'll help you relax.

69. W: Hello, may I speak with Mr. Jimenez?
     M: I'm sorry he's with a client.
     W: This is Bill Carter. He's half an hour late for our appointment.

70. W: I've tried everything, but my computer isn't working.
     M: Is there anything on the screen?
     W: Lots of numbers and abbreviations that I don't understand.

71. W: How much longer is the exhibit at the Science Museum going to be in town?
     M: It's definitely leaving September first. No more extensions.
     W: So will you go with me Wednesday evening? I heard it's not as crowded then as on the weekends.

72. M: As long as we're reprinting the brochure, why don't we think about making a five-minute video that we could send out to prospective customers?
     W: Great idea! Can you get some estimates by the end of the week?
     M: Yeah, sure. I saw one that was fantastic last week.

73. W: Can you find out how long Ann is going to be out?
     M: I'll call and ask her. I heard she's got the flu.
     W: We'll need to bring in a temporary receptionist. We can't keep asking Judy to sit downstairs.

74. W: Is there a train for Berlin that leaves on Tuesday after 3:00?
     M: I'll check. There's one at 4:00.
     W: Good. I have a meeting at noon which shouldn't take more than an hour.

75. W: Did you see in the paper that Panther Publishing has decided to stay in its downtown location?
     M: I thought they were considering buying the old Foster Mill.
     W: The Mill is larger, but it sounds like most of the employees fought hard to stay where they are.

76. M: Did you know that all hotels built after 1985 have to have automomatic sprinklers in every room?
     W: What about older ones?
     M: They have until March of next year to install them.

77. W: I haven't seen Patty Williams at the health club or in the cafeteria for a while.
     M: I heard she took a leave of absence from the accounting department.
     W: Oh yeah. I remember she said she wanted to try and get that tax book written.

78. M: How is this merit system going to work?
     W: In addition to annual pay raises, your supervisor can recommend you for a merit raise.
     M: What happens if you don't get one, but you think you should?

79. W: I wish I had known your meeting was in Switzerland.
     M: I thought you knew.
     W: No, and it's the only place I can get the chocolates I love.

80. M: Aren't you the export director? I'm David Chan, the new V.P. for sales.
     W: You look awfully familiar. Did we meet at the Belgium Trade Fair last year?
     M: Yes, I was talking with your supervisor who introduced us.

Questions 81–83 refer to the following announcement:

W: The company's annual picnic will be held at the PineBrook Country Club on Thursday, July 27 from 12:00–4:00 in the afternoon. All employees are invited to bring their spouses and children. Please call Joyce Chen at extension 2385 to RSVP by July 25. We will be able to use all of the club's facilities, so bring your bathing suits, tennis rackets, and golf clubs! Lunch will be served at 1:00. Buses will depart from the west parking lot at 11:30 sharp. You may drive yourselves if you wish, but please notify Ms. Chen if you will not be taking the bus.

Questions 84–86 refer to the following speech:

M1: As many of you know, two weeks ago Friday was the national competition deadline to name our company's mascot. Our cute teddy bear, which adorns all of our products' boxes, has been nameless since its creation twenty-five years ago. The response to this campaign was simply overwhelming. We received over seventeen thousand entries. Each sender, of course, is hoping to win the ten-thousand dollar prize. Our staff of ten has miraculously selected twenty semifinalists. We are asking all of you to stop by the cafeteria sometime this week and pick up an official ballot form and choose the name you like best. Please write your name on the ballot and vote only once. Thank you all in advance for your participation.

Questions 87–89 refer to the following talk:

M2: Ladies and gentlemen, gold prices opened in London this morning at a twenty-year low of $318.00 per ounce. At this time we are advising our clients to hold onto their gold, for our analysts conclude that prices have bottomed out. However, we should begin to see increasing gold prices after the first of the year.

Questions 90–91 refer to the following report:

W: Our marketing director, Gayle Forsyth, was seriously injured in a car accident yesterday afternoon while returning home from a vacation in Montreal. She was driving on Route 87 when she struck a moose which had strayed onto the highway. She was airlifted to the Dartmouth Medical Facility where she remains in critical condition. The hospital has asked us not to send flowers at this time. We will update you on her progress.

Questions 92–94 refer to the following advertisement:

M2: Fly as our air messenger, and you can save up to eighty percent on international travel. It's the cheapest way to fly to Europe, Asia, Mexico, Central and South America, and the Pacific Rim. We arrange over seven hundred one-way and round-trip flights weekly. You must be twenty-one or over, have documentation of a recent physical examination, possess a valid passport, and be willing to jump aboard a flight at the last minute. Give us a call today!

Questions 95–97 refer to the following announcement:

M1: In response to numerous customer complaints, we are updating our phone reservation service. Although we have ten different phone lines, customers have been complaining about dialing for an hour or more and getting a busy signal at each try. Beginning on Monday, we will add fifteen new lines. However, the increase in the number of lines will not necessitate additional employees.

Questions 98–100 refer to the following announcement:

W: The real estate division of Front Row Properties, International, has announced a joint venture with Pattaya Development Corporation to develop a strip of land along the coastline in the northern part of the city. The proposed project, which still needs the approval of the city building commission, will include high-rise luxury apartments, a two-hundred-room five-star hotel, shopping areas, and recreational facilities. The architecture firm of Diamond, Black, and Epp, which has designed similar projects throughout the Far East, will submit its plans in two weeks.

1. (B) *People are crossing the street in the crosswalk.*
Choice (A) is incorrect because the light is to the right of the direction signs. Choice (C) is incorrect because there are no cars in the crosswalk. Choice (D) is incorrect because the pedestrians are not waiting; they are crossing the street.

2. (C) *People are eating in front of the restaurant.*
Choice (A) is incorrect because they are sitting on chairs, not benches. Choice (B) is incorrect because food is being served outside. Choice (D) is incorrect because the restaurant is open.

3. (A) *The man is just about to kick the ball.*
Choice (B) is incorrect because the man is standing. Choice (C) is incorrect because the man is not near any other player. Choice (D) is incorrect because the ball is on the ground.

4. (D) *The man's eyes aren't visible because of the sunglasses.*
Choice (A) is incorrect because the man is not holding back the people. Choice (B) is incorrect because the man is already wearing sunglasses. Choice (C) is incorrect because the man's arms are folded.

5. (A) *A man and woman are shaking hands.*
Choice (B) is incorrect because a man is shaking hands with a woman. Choice (C) is incorrect because there is no other woman in the picture. Choice (D) is incorrect because a woman and man are greeting each other.

6. (D) *One of the waiters has not put on a bow tie.*
Choice (A) is incorrect because the men are posing for a picture, not looking for a job. Choice (B) is incorrect because one of the waiters is not wearing a bow tie. Choice (C) is incorrect because the men are posing for a picture, not working.

7. (D) *The skiers are waiting in line.*
Choice (A) is incorrect because the skiers' masks are not covering their faces. Choice (B) is incorrect because the skiers are holding their skis. Choice (C) is incorrect because the skiers are outdoors, not checking into the lodge.

8. (A) *A lot of smoke is coming out of the factory's chimneys.*
Choice (B) is incorrect because there are no clouds in the sky. Choice (C) is incorrect because the factory is open, producing smoke. Choice (D) is incorrect because there are no smokers in the picture, only smoke.

9. (C) *The girl is studying on a bench outdoors.*
Choice (A) is incorrect because the girl is studying, not shopping. Choice (B) is incorrect because she has her study materials with her. Choice (D) is incorrect because the girl is sitting, not moving a bench.

10. (B) *The men are painting the outside of the building.*
Choice (A) is incorrect because the building is being painted, not demolished. Choice (C) is incorrect because the painters are painting the outside of the building, not the inside. Choice (D) is incorrect because the men are standing on a plank, not ladders.

11. (D) *The two girls are eating ice cream outdoors.*
Choice (A) is incorrect because they are not climbing a tree. Choice (B) is incorrect because they are eating ice cream, not buying it. Choice (C) is incorrect because they are both eating ice cream, not sharing it with other people.

12. (D) *The flags are flying above the Palace Hotel sign.*
Choice (A) is incorrect because there is no advertising of an opening. Choice (B) is incorrect because there is no doorman visible in the picture. Choice (C) is incorrect because the flags are not next to the entrance, but above the hotel.

13. (A) *Many people are crossing the street.*
Choice (B) is incorrect because the people are already walking, not waiting. Choice (C) is incorrect because there are no cars in the picture. Choice (D) is incorrect because the people are crossing, not standing.

14. (B) *The bullfighter is waving a flag in front of the bull.*
Choice (A) is incorrect because the bull is approaching the bullfighter. Choice (C) is incorrect because the bullfighter is bending, not kneeling. Choice (D) is incorrect because the bull is already in the ring.

15. (C) *People are clapping.*
Choice (A) is incorrect because the man in the glasses is clapping, not performing. Choice (B) is incorrect because the spectators are appreciative, not amused. Choice (D) is incorrect because the spectators are at a performance; it has not been canceled.

16. (A) *Some passengers are exiting the airport with their luggage.*
Choice (B) is incorrect because the luggage has been removed from the plane. Choice (C) is incorrect because some passengers have already gotten their luggage. Choice (D) is incorrect because the carousel must be working if some passengers have their luggage.

17. (C) *The hotel clerk is checking something, presumably a reservation, for the guest.*
Choice (A) is incorrect because the clerk is not lifting the keyboard. Choice (B) is incorrect because the clerk is not making change. Choice (D) is incorrect because there are no keys visible in the picture.

18. (C) *The man and woman are washing dishes.*
Choice (A) is incorrect because there is no dishwasher in the picture. Choice (B) is incorrect because the couple are washing dishes, not setting the table. Choice (D) is incorrect because the couple are not cooking; they are washing.

19. (B) *The woman is paying for her lunch.*
Choice (A) is incorrect because there are no waiters in the picture. Choices (C) and (D) are incorrect because the woman already has her food.

20. (A) *The referee is blowing the whistle.*
Choices (B) and (C) are incorrect because the whistle is already in his mouth. Choice (D) is incorrect because there are no players in the picture.

21. (C) *I left it on your desk* answers where Carlos put the report that he finished. Choice (A) answers the question *What do you do?* Choice (B) is often said as a goodbye, meaning *I'll see you again tomorrow.*

22. (B) *In the hotel room* answers where the speaker saw the passport. Choice (A) answers the question *Where did you get your passport?* Choice (C) answers *Where are you going?*

23. (A) *I had to do the books,* meaning *I was working on the accounts,* explains why the speaker couldn't go to the party. Choice (B) answers a question such as *When did you give Joseph the gift?* Choice (C) answers the question *Do you like parties?*

24. (C) *No, I do everything myself* indicates that the speaker does not have a typist and does all the typing by herself. Choice (A) answers the question *Would you like some* (coffee, etc.)? Choice (B) answers a question such as *Do you want a* (noun)?

25. (B) *Six months* answers how long the speaker has lived in this country. Choice (A) answers a question such as *When will you be going to Europe again?* Choice (C) answers a *when* question using the simple past.

26. (A) *I'm the new marketing director* affirms that the speaker got the promotion. Choices (B) and (C) are illogical responses.

27. (C) *That's Mr. Chan's job* explains who orders new software. Choice (A) answers a *where* question. Choice (B) is an illogical response.

28. (B) *If it's OK with you, I'd rather leave later* means the speaker would prefer leaving at 8:00, not at 7:00. Choice (A) confuses *8:00* with *ate.* Choice (C) answers a *when* question using the simple past.

29. (C) *I didn't know he had so much to say* confirms the speaker's surprise that *he spoke for so long.* Choices (A) and (B) are illogical responses.

30. (A) *As long as you wear a suit* means it's all right if he doesn't wear a tie, but he must at least wear a suit. Choice (B) confuses *tie* with *tied up.* Choice (C) is an illogical response.

31. (B) *I traded weeks with Steven* means he exchanged vacation weeks so that he could take two weeks off at one time. Choice (A) confuses *manage* with *manager.* Choice (C) answers a *where* question.

32. (A) *I hope next week* answers when he plans to hire a new employee. Choice (B) confuses *filling* with *feeling.* Choice (C) confuses *opening* with *close.*

33. (C) *No, go right ahead* means it's OK with the woman if the man watches her. Choices (A) and (B) are illogical responses.

34. (B) *The same as last month* means that the sales quota has not changed. Choice (A) is an illogical response. Choice (C) answers the question *how many times.*

35. (C) *I know she's planning to* means he knows Mrs. Suzuki wants to register, although she may not have done so yet. Choice (A) answers the question *when.* Choice (B) answers the question *how often.*

36. (A) *I thought he said he'd let us know* means the woman understood that the lawyer will inform them of his decision. Choice (B) answers *Is the lawyer going to tell us?* Choice (C) answers a *where* question.

37. (C) *We've been asked to bring in our own reusable cups* explains what happened to all the cups; disposable cups will no longer be supplied. Choice (A) confuses *coffee cups* and *china cups.* Choice (B) answers the question *how many.*

38. (B) *I thought it had been postponed* explains why the man wasn't at the meeting. Choice (A) answers the question *when.* Choice (C) answers *Will you be at the department meeting?*

39. (A) *Actually, what's more important is the price* explains that the woman's top priority is how much the car costs, not whether it has two or four doors. Choice (B) answers *how many.* Choice (C) is an illogical response.

40. (B) *Not before the first of the month* indicates that documents won't be translated before the first day of the next month. Choices (A) and (C) respond to the question *How long will you be in town?*

41. (C) *I need to speak to him* means the woman must speak to Mr. Young and cannot leave a message. Choice (A) answers the question *Can you wait for Mr. Young?* Choice (B) confuses *take* with *taken.*

42. (C) *I haven't had a minute to look it over* means the speaker cannot give his opinion of the proposal because he's been too busy to look at it. Choice (A) answers the question *Can you look at the proposal?* Choice (B) answers the question *How long have you been engaged?*

43. (A) *No, I work on the eighth* means she's not the new employee who works on the fifth floor; she works on the eighth floor. Choice (B) confuses the *fifth floor* with *leaving on the fifth.* Choice (C) is an illogical response.

44. (C) *I think it's Peter Newport, but you'd better check* means the speaker thinks Peter Newport is the one who is responsible for sales for Seoul. Choice (A) answers the question *Where are the Korean reports?* Choice (B) is an illogical response.

45. (C) *By twenty-five percent* indicates how much the product will be discounted. Choice (A) answers a *how many* question. Choice (B) is an illogical response.

46. (B) *I'm not too good with punctuation* means he'll proofread the memo, but he may not be able to correct the punctuation. Choice (A) is an illogical response. Choice (C) answers the question *Did you read the memo?*

47. (A) *At the duty-free shop at the airport* tells where the woman bought her briefcase. Choice (B) confuses *brief* and *not long.* Choice (C) answers the question *Is that a vinyl briefcase?*

48. (C) *No, I'm happy working here* means the man has not sent out resumes to other companies because he likes his job. Choice (A) answers a *were you* question. Choice (B) confuses the noun *resumes* with the verb *resume.*

49. (B) *A taxi is quicker but more expensive* gives the speaker's opinion of whether the man should take a cab or bus to the airport. Choice (A) answers a *can I* question. Choice (C) is not a response to a choice question.

50. (A) *In high school* explains where the speaker learned to speak German. Choices (B) and (C) are illogical responses.

51. (C) The woman asks *Could you stop by my apartment and water my plants?* Choice (A) confuses the woman's saying she *had the locks changed* with *change her lock.* Choice (B) confuses that the woman, not the man, is going to the conference. The man already has the woman's key, so they don't need to exchange keys, Choice (D).

52. (B) Jack asks *what form* he's *supposed to use.* Choice (A) is incorrect; he does not say that he cannot find her. Choice (C) is incorrect; the woman tells him that Ms. Williams must sign the form, but that is not the problem. Choice (D) is incorrect because it is clear that he knows office expenses are reimbursable.

53. (D) The man asks *Have you ever taken the subway to work?* Choice (A) is contradicted by his saying he heard *the expressway is being rerouted for the next two weeks.* Choices (B) and (C) are not mentioned.

54. (A) The woman says that yesterday *her computer took an hour to pull up the addresses* she needed, meaning *it worked slowly.* Choice (B) confuses *hot weather* with *overheated.* Choice (C) is not mentioned. Choice (D) is contradicted by *her computer took an hour to pull up the addresses.*

55. (C) The woman says *tell me what you'd like and I'll bring it back for you,* meaning she'll bring him back lunch. Choice (A) is not mentioned. She does not suggest Choice (B); she asks him if he's *going out for lunch.* Choice (D) is not mentioned.

56. (B) *The personnel office doesn't have a copy of* Michael's resume and he needs to get one to *Kathy Jones by the end of the week.* Although he already brought one, it's *no problem to print another one.* Choices (A), (C), and (D) are not mentioned.

57. (A) Mrs. Yee was told *her flight would be direct from Los Angeles,* but *there was a four-hour stopover in Hawaii.* Choice (B) is incorrect; she didn't miss her connection. Choice (C) is incorrect; she wasn't told about a stopover in Hawaii. Choice (D) is not mentioned.

58. (D) The woman asks the man *Will you be going straight from work?,* meaning she wonders if he will go home before the party or go to the party directly from work. Choice (A) confuses engagement party with wedding. Choices (B) and (C) are not mentioned.

59. (C) The man asks if she *noticed how much cleaner everything looks around here.* Choice (A) is not mentioned. Although the man's computer screen was cleaned, he did not get a new one, making Choice (B) incorrect. Choice (D) is not mentioned.

60. (B) The woman says *I've asked everyone else in the office,* meaning the conversation took place at the office. Choice (A) confuses the subject *recommending a dentist* with where the conversation took place, *the office*. Choice (C) confuses where Brian, the dentist, practices, with where the conversation took place. Choice (D) is incorrect; it confuses how old Brian looks (seventeen) with the location of the conversation.

61. (D) The woman says *Is it the documents from Jakarta? Mr. Palmer has been waiting for this.* Although the packages are from New York, Zurich, and Australia, they're not what Mr. Palmer has been waiting for, making Choices (A), (B), and (C) incorrect.

62. (A) The woman says that during the first week in August *no one will be in the office, but the shipping department will be working.* Choice (B) confuses *told me* with *Toby.* Choice (C) isn't mentioned. The shipping department will be filling back orders, but no mention is made of how long that will take, making Choice (D) incorrect.

63. (C) The man asks if *the company is still looking for a legal consultant.* Choice (A) confuses *patent expertise* with *patent.* The man recommends *Gray and Kanter;* he doesn't ask if they've been hired, making Choice (B) incorrect. Choice (D) confuses *international patent lawyer* with *international.*

64. (B) The woman says *then we'll only need about ten* (more chairs). Choice (A) confuses *sixth floor* and *6.* Choice (C) is not mentioned. Choice (D) confuses the number of chairs they already have with the number they'll need.

65. (A) Joe says *I thought it might be a good place to take the consultants,* meaning a place to entertain visitors. Choices (B) and (C) are not mentioned. Choice (D) confuses *the home office* with *close to home.*

66. (D) The man tells Shell International that *there'll be an additional charge for each change made.* Choice (A) confuses *the goods* with *the charges.* Choice (B) is contradicted by *there'll be an additional charge for each change made.* Choice (C) is said by the woman.

67. (C) The man says he wants to tell the decorators when *they can see it,* meaning visit the building. Choice (A) is not mentioned. Choice (B) is not done by the decorators, but by the lawyers. Choice (D) is not mentioned.

68. (B) The man says he's *got a great book* for her to take on her trip. Choice (A) is what Monica says she has to do. Choices (C) and (D) are not mentioned.

69. (A) Bill Carter says that Mr. Jimenez is *half an hour late for our appointment.* Choices (B), (C), and (D) are not mentioned.

70. (B) The woman says *her computer isn't working.* Choice (A) is not mentioned. Choice (C) confuses *TV screen* with *computer screen.* Choice (D) is not mentioned.

71. (D) The woman asks *So will you go with me on Wednesday evening?* Choice (A) is incorrect because September 1st is the day the exhibit is leaving. Choice (B) is not mentioned. Choice (C) is incorrect because it is mentioned as a time when the museum is crowded.

72. (C) The man says *Why don't we think about making a five-minute video?* Choice (A) is incorrect because the brochures are already being reprinted; it's not his proposal. Choice (B) is not mentioned. Choice (D) confuses getting *some estimates by the end of the week* with *sending out materials this week.*

73. (A) The woman says *we can't keep asking Judy to sit downstairs* where she is currently replacing Ann. Choice (B) is not mentioned. Choice (C) is incorrect because it is Ann, not Judy, who has the flu. Choice (D) confuses *upstairs* and *downstairs.*

74. (D) The man says *there's one* (a train) *at four.* Choice (A) confuses the time of the meeting with the train's departure time. Choice (B) confuses *there's one* with *one o'clock.* Choice (C) is incorrect; the woman asks if there is a train after 3:00.

75. (B) The woman says *the mill is larger.* Choice (A) is incorrect; the size, not the location, is the reason they were considering moving. Choice (C) is contradicted by *the employees fought hard to stay where they are.* Choice (D) is where Panther Publishing is now located, not where the old Foster Mill is.

76. (C) The man says that hotels built before 1985 *have until March of next year to install* automatic sprinklers. Choice (A) is incorrect; they will need to have sprinkler systems installed. Choice (B) is incorrect; they are discussing the installation of sprinkler systems in these hotels. Choice (D) is incorrect because hotels *have until March of next year.*

77. (D) The man says he heard Patty Williams *took a leave from the accounting department;* she's an accountant. Choices (A) and (B) are incorrect; they confuse the jobs *fitness instructor* and *cafeteria worker* with places Patty was sometimes seen — the *health club* and the *cafeteria.* Choice (C) confuses writing a book with being an editor.

78. (A) The man asks *What happens if you don't get one* (a merit raise), *but you think you should?* Choices (B), (C), and (D) are not mentioned.

79. (C) The woman says she wishes she *had known* the man's *meeting was in Switzerland.* Choices (A) and (B) are not mentioned. Choice (D) is incorrect because the woman had wanted the man to get something, not send something.

80. (B) The man asks the woman *Aren't you the export director?* Choice (A) is incorrect because she says that David's supervisor introduced them. Choice (C) is incorrect because it confuses *organizing* trade fairs as a job with *attending* trade fairs as a participant. Choice (D) is incorrect because the man is *the new VP for sales.*

81. (C) The announcement begins *The company's annual picnic will be held...* Choice (A) is not mentioned. Although the time of the bus departure is mentioned, the route is not, making Choice (B) incorrect. Choice (D) is not mentioned.

82. (B) The *picnic will be held from 12:00–4:00;* starting at 12:00. Choice (A) is incorrect because that is the time the buses will depart. Choice (C) is incorrect because that is the time lunch will be served. Choice (D) is incorrect because that is when the picnic will end.

83. (A) *Please call Joyce Chen... to RSVP by July 25.* Choice (B) is the date of the picnic. Choice (C) is the time that the buses depart. Choice (D) is not mentioned.

84. (D) The speech begins *two weeks ago Friday was the national competition deadline to name our company's mascot; the cute teddy bear, which adorns all of our product's boxes, has been nameless for twenty-five years.* Choice (A) is incorrect because there has been a mascot for twenty-five years. Choices (B) and (C) are not mentioned.

85. (C) The speech continues *we received over seventeen thousand entries.* Choice (A) is incorrect because it is the number of years the teddy bear has been nameless. Choice (B) is incorrect because it is the dollar amount of the prize. Choice (D) confuses the twenty semifinalists with twenty thousand.

86. (A) Employees are asked *to stop by the cafeteria sometime this week and pick up an official ballot form and choose the name you like best.* Choice (B) is incorrect because the staff of ten selected twenty semi-finalists from the over seventeen thousand entries. Choices (C) and (D) are not mentioned.

87. (B) The talk begins *gold prices opened at a twenty-year low.* Choice (A) is not mentioned. Choice (C) is incorrect because prices should begin to rise after the first of the year. Choice (D) is not mentioned.

88. (A) Clients are being advised *to hold onto their gold, which means to wait and not sell.* Choices (B), (C), and (D) are contradicted by *clients are being advised to hold onto their gold.*

89. (D) *We should begin to see increasing gold prices after the first of the year.* Choices (A), (B), and (C) are contradicted by *we should begin to see increasing gold prices after the first of the year.*

90. (A) The announcement begins *Our marketing director, Gayle Forsyth, was seriously injured in a car accident yesterday...* Choice (B) is incorrect; she is not dead but is in critical condition. Choice (C) is not mentioned although the report asks that no flowers be sent. Choice (D) mentions the route she was driving on but it is not the main purpose of the announcement.

91. (D) The accident was caused when Ms. Forsyth's car *struck a moose.* Choice (A) is not mentioned. Choice (B) confuses *airlifted* with *airplane.* Choice (C) is not mentioned or implied.

92. (B) The advertisement begins *fly as our air messenger, and you can save up to eighty percent on international travel.* Choices (A), (C), and (D) are not mentioned.

93. (D) The advertisement says *fly as our air messenger,* it's a courier service. Choices (A), (B), and (C) are not mentioned.

94. (C) *We arrange over seven hundred one-way and round-trip flights weekly.* Choice (A) is incorrect because it confuses the age one must be. Choice (B) is incorrect because it confuses the percent one can save. Choice (D) is incorrect because it doubles the number of weekly flights.

95. (B) *Beginning on Monday, we will add fifteen new* (phone) *lines.* Choice (A) confuses *installing a telephone* with *adding lines.* Choice (C) is incorrect; no one will be hired and there are no new hiring procedures. Choice (D) confuses *customer inquiries* with *customer complaints.*

96. (C) *Beginning on Monday, we will add fifteen new lines.* Choice (A) is incorrect because *the increase in the number of lines will not necessitate additional employees.* Choice (B) is not mentioned. New phone lines are being added because customers have complained about getting busy signals, but no mention is made of eliminating the busy signal entirely; therefore, Choice (D) is incorrect.

97. (C) *We have ten lines... beginning on Monday, we will add fifteen new lines,* which makes twenty-five lines. Choice (A) is incorrect because it confuses the number of existing lines. Choice (B) is incorrect because it confuses the number of additional lines. Choice (D) is not mentioned.

98. (D) The announcement details *a joint venture to develop a strip of land,* meaning a development project. Choices (A), (B), and (C) are not mentioned.

99. (B) *The project will include luxury apartments, a hotel, shopping areas, and recreational facilities;* a coastline marina is not mentioned. Choices (A), (C), and (D) are explicitly mentioned.

100. (C) *The firm of Diamond, Black, and Epp has designed similar projects...* Choices (A), (B), and (D) are not mentioned.

101. (C) The relationship in these two independent clauses is one of opposition because they are connected by *but; neither* shows a contrast. Choices (A), (B), and (D) do not show a contrast.

102. (B) *The greater,* the comparative form, is parallel to *the more pressure.* Choice (A) is the superlative form. Choices (C) and (D) are incorrect.

103. (D) *Divide one number by another.* Choices (A), (B), and (C) are not used with *divide.*

104. (A) *He cut his hair by himself; himself* is the reflexive form. Choice (B) is the object pronoun. Choice (C) is an incorrect word. Choice (D) is the possessive pronoun.

105. (C) *Acceptable* means *satisfactory.* Choice (A) is an adverb, which cannot follow a linking verb. Choice (B) means *possessing additional items that add to an overall effect.* Choice (D) means *answerable.*

106. (C) The causative verb *had* is followed by the doer, *the travel agency,* and the base form, *make.* Choices (A), (B), and (D) are followed by the infinitive form of the verb.

107. (A) The adjective form *continuous* precedes the compound noun *airmail service.* Choices (B), (C), and (D) are nouns.

108. (D) *Together,* the adverb, follows the direct object *lunch.* Choices (A) and (B) are adjectives. Choice (C) is a preposition.

109. (B) *Despite,* a preposition, precedes the noun *cost.* Choice (A) needs to be followed by *of.* Choice (C) must be followed by a subject + verb. Choice (D) cannot be followed by an object.

110. (C) *Come up with* means *create* or *design.* Choices (A) and (B) mean *visit.* Choice (D) means *return.*

111. (A) The adjective form *wide* modifies *highway* and follows the measurement *three and a half meters.* Choice (B) is a noun. Choice (C) is an adverb. Choice (D) is a verb.

112. (B) The noun *snowstorm* follows the article *a.* Choice (A) is an adjective. Choice (C) is a gerund. Choice (D) is illogical.

113. (C) Only persons, *accountants,* can be employed. Choices (A) and (B) are noun things. Choice (D) is an adjective.

114. (D) *Seven days a week* is an expression meaning *every day.* Choices (A), (B), and (C) are not logical.

115. (A) *Break down* means *fail to function.* Choice (B) means *divide.* Choice (C) means *begin suddenly.* Choice (D) means *make a sudden quick advance.*

116. (C) The noun *investigation* follows the preposition *under.* Choice (A) is a person noun. Choice (B) is an adjective or a gerund form. Choice (D) is a verb.

117. (B) The possessive pronoun *whose* precedes the noun *desk* to show possession. Choice (A) is a subject pronoun. Choice (C) is used only before nouns in the question form. Choice (D) is illogical.

118. (D) The adjective *alike,* meaning *similar,* follows a linking verb. Choice (A) would not follow a negative word, *nothing.* Choice (B) is an adverb meaning *probable.* Choice (C) is either a verb or a preposition.

119. (A) The correct word order is preposition, *due to;* possessive pronoun, *his;* noun, *lack;* preposition, *of;* noun, *experience.* Choices (B), (C), and (D) are in the wrong order.

120. (C) *All-time* is an adjective, preceding the noun *high.* Choices (A), (B), and (D) are adverbs.

121. (D) *With many branches nationwide* means *with many branches which are located throughout the nation;* the relative pronoun and verb have been deleted. Choice (A) is a verb. Choice (B) is an adjective which must precede a noun. Choice (C) is a noun.

122. (B) *Rotate* means *exchange.* Choice (A) is not logical. Choice (C) does not precede nouns. Choice (D) is not logical.

123. (A) *Second,* an adjective, with its adverb modifier *only,* follows the linking verb, *is.* Choices (B), (C), and (D) are not logical.

124. (D) *On second thought* means *after reconsideration.* Choice (A) introduces an independent clause. Choices (B) and (C) are not logical.

125. (C) *Flight attendants* is a correct plural compound noun. Choices (A) and (D) incorrectly use an apostrophe + *s* to form the compound noun. Choice (B) incorrectly uses the plural form for the word *flight,* used here as an adjective in the compound noun.

126. (D) The past modal form, *should have made,* is needed in this sentence. Choice (A) is the past modal passive form. Choice (B) is the present tense passive form. Choice (C), *made,* cannot follow *should.*

127. (C) The conjunction *or* indicates a choice, so payments can be made *every other month,* meaning *every second month.* Choice (A) means the same as *monthly.* Choices (B) and (D) are not logical.

128. (A) *Look through* means *examine.* Choice (B), although meaning *examine,* is used for a location, not an article such as a *brochure.* Choice (C) means *anticipate.* Choice (D) means *respect.*

129. (B) *On the average* is a prepositional phrase meaning *usually.* Choices (A), (C), and (D) cannot be set off with a comma.

130. (D) *The model was inferior to the old one.* Choices (A) and (B) must be followed by *than,* not *to.* Choice (C) is a preposition and must be followed by a noun, not *to.*

131. (A) *Another opening* means *an additional opening.* Choice (B), when used without a preceding *the,* must be followed by a plural noun or a noncount noun. Choice (C), a pronoun, cannot be followed by a noun. Choice (D), an adjective, *other,* and a pronoun, *ones,* cannot be followed by a noun.

132. (B) *Bidding a fond farewell* means *saying a warm goodbye.* Choices (A), (C), and (D) are not logical in this sentence.

133. (B) The passive form, *be alphabetized,* is needed in this sentence. Choice (A) is the active present tense. Choice (C) completes the infinitive with *be* + the present participle. Choice (D) is an adjective.

134. (C) *The agents who had the highest gross profits* are the employees who made the most money. Choices (A) and (D) would not be used with people. Choice (B) is not logical.

135. (D) *On time* is an idiom meaning *on schedule.* Choices (A), (B), and (C) are not logical.

136. (B) The pronoun *mine* is used to show possession when there is no noun following it. Choice (A) must be followed by a noun. Choice (C) is the object pronoun. Choice (D) is the reflexive pronoun.

137. (D) The correct word order is verb, *put;* preposition, *in;* article, *a;* adjective, *good;* noun, *word;* meaning *say good things about you.* Choices (A), (B), and (C) are in the wrong order.

138. (A) When the verb *recommend* is followed by a dependent clause, the simple form of the verb, *get,* must follow the subject. Choice (B) is the simple present tense. Choice (C) is the present continuous tense. Choice (D) is the future tense.

139. (B) The correct phrase is *ten years ago.* Choices (A), (C), and (D) are not logical.

140. (C) *Single or double occupancy* means *being one guest or two.* Choice (A) is not logical. Choice (B) is a single count noun and must be preceded by an article. Choice (D) is not logical.

141. (B) *Both... and* is a paired conjunction; *both print advertisements and radio announcements.*

142. (C) The past tense form is needed: *began.*

143. (C) The passive form of the verb is needed: *has been dipped.*

144. (C) For two items the preposition *between* should be used — *between a tangerine and a grapefruit.*

145. (A) *No,* used as an adjective, should precede the subject pronoun, *one.*

146. (B) The correct superlative form is *largest.*

147. (D) Use an adjective before a noun: *continuous lengths.*

148. (A) The adverb form is needed before a verb: *easily.*

149. (B) *Because* introduces a clause of describing a *cause.* In this sentence *because* is introducing a clause of effect, and thus makes the sentence illogical. *Because* should be deleted.

150. (D) The plural form of *regulation* should be used — *more than five hundred pages of customs and tariff regulations.*

151. (B) The adverb form should precede a verb: *totally.*

152. (A) *He* is not necessary because the sentence already has a subject: *Mr. Lucas Jones.*

153. (D) *Surprising and unexpected* gives the same information and is redundant; either one word or the other should be used.

154. (D) The adjective form is required; *economic* makes this sentence parallel.

155. (D) *Easier* is the correct comparative form.

156. (B) The correct intransitive verb is *rises; raises* takes a direct object.

157. (D) The correct expression is *making progress.*

158. (C) The passive form of the verb is needed: *considered.*

159. (D) The preposition is incorrect; *by* should be used.

160. (D) The noun form is needed: *weight.*

161. (B) *Marketing* is one of the concentrations mentioned. Choices (A), (C), and (D) are not mentioned.

162. (C) *Advanced standing credit may reduce the amount of time needed to complete the program. Advanced standing credit* means *credits transferred from another institution.* Choice (A) is incorrect because one doesn't reduce the time needed *only* by taking one-week courses. Choices (B) and (D) are not mentioned.

163. (A) *For more information... call us.* Choices (B), (C), and (D) are not mentioned.

164. (D) The company is *currently exporting to Asia,* so Seoul is where this company might do business. Choices (A), (B), and (C) are not where the company currently exports.

165. (C) The company manufactures *comforter sets*; *sheets* are a part of these sets. Choices (A), (B), and (D) are not mentioned.

166. (B) *A representative of the company will be visiting the U.S. at the end of July.* Choices (A), (C), and (D) are contradicted by *visiting the U.S.*

167. (A) *Send us your salary requirements,* meaning *desired wages.* Choices (B), (C), and (D) are not mentioned.

168. (C) *On Friday, the Brazilian stock market was flat,* meaning *unchanged.* Choice (A) is incorrect because only *telecommunications and banking stocks continued their upward trend.* Choices (B) and (D) are not mentioned.

169. (B) *Investors stayed on the sidelines waiting for large players to make their next moves.* Choice (A) is not mentioned. Choice (C) has already happened. Choice (D) is not mentioned.

170. (D) *Cash-rich domestic pension-fund managers bought up stocks.* Choices (A), (B), and (C) are contradicted by *cash-rich domestic pension-fund managers.*

171. (A) *Enjoy swimming...* Choices (B), (C), and (D) are not mentioned.

172. (C) *On board are 74 luxurious cabins, each facing the sea.* Choices (A), (B), and (D) are not mentioned.

173. (B) There is *a staff of 88.* Choice (A) is the number of cabins. Choice (C) is not mentioned. Choice (D) is the number of feet of the cruise ship.

174. (C) *Take a 12-, 14-, or 21-day cruise;* the maximum number of weeks is three (21 days). Choices (A), (B), and (D) are contradicted by *21 days.*

175. (D) The exhibit will *surprise visitors* with Picasso's *sculptures.* Choices (A), (B), and (C) are not mentioned.

176. (C) *The exhibit will delight visitors with well-known examples of Picasso's work from his Blue and Rose Periods.* Choice (A) is contradicted by *each ticket will be issued for a specific half-hour of entry.* Although *tickets go on sale on July 15,* Choice (B), the exhibit opens on *September 15.* Choice (D) is contradicted by *well-known examples of Picasso's work from his Blue and Rose Periods,* which occurred sometime between 1892-1906, the years of the exhibit.

177. (D) A large turnout is anticipated *for this special two-month exhibit;* the exhibit opens in mid-September and will close in mid-November. Choices (A), (B), and (C) are contradicted by *this special two-month exhibit.*

178. (B) The announcement is entitled *Health Insurance Changes* and describes the employee benefits. Choices (A) and (C) are not mentioned. Choice (D) is incorrect because there is only one dental plan mentioned.

179. (C) *Single employees will pay 10% of the costs,* so if the plan costs $2,000, the employee would contribute $200. Choices (A), (B), and (D) are contradicted by *single employees will pay 10% of the costs.*

180. (D) The paragraph addresses *employees,* meaning *company workers.* Choice (A) is not mentioned. Choice (B) is mentioned, but married employees are also addressed in the *family plan* coverage. Although the paragraph describes different *medical insurers,* Choice (C), *employees* are being addressed.

181. (A) *Effective with the calendar year of 1999, every new employee must choose Pilgrim Health Plan.* Choices (B), (C), and (D) are contradicted by *effective with the calendar year of 1999, every new employee must choose Pilgrim Health Plan.*

182. (D) *The B.A. Beagle Company announced higher-than-expected profits for the second quarter ending July 31;* therefore, the announcement was made after July 31. Choices (A), (B), and (C) are contradicted by *The B.A. Beagle Company announced higher-than-expected profits for the second quarter ending July 31.*

183. (B) *The higher-than-expected profits,* due to *cost-cutting measures, caused the stock to rise; cost-cutting measures* are a reduction in expenses. Choices (A), (C), and (D) are contradicted by *the higher-than-expected profits, due to cost-cutting measures, caused the stock to rise.*

184. (C) *President A. J. Donaldson arrived in January of last year;* therefore, he has been with the company *at least a year.* Choices (A), (B), and (D) are contradicted by *President A. J. Donaldson arrived in January of last year.*

185. (A) *The highway department announced the closing of two... lanes... for repair work.* Choice (B) is not mentioned. Choice (C) is contradicted by *the speed limit will be reduced.* Choice (D) is not mentioned.

186. (C) *There are four lanes in each direction;* therefore, there are eight lanes. Choices (A), (B), and (D) are contradicted by *there are four lanes in each direction.*

187. (D) *The speed limit... will be strictly enforced by the police.* Choices (A), (B), and (C) are contradicted by *the speed limit... will be strictly enforced by the police.*

188. (C) *Traffic to Route 135 will use Exit 41,* a different exit. Choice (A) is incorrect because the Exit is 41, not 40. Choices (B) and (D) are contradicted by *traffic to Route 135 will use Exit 41.*

189. (C) *This agreement... is governed in accordance with the laws of the Republic of Singapore.* Choices (A), (B), and (D) are contradicted by *this agreement... is governed in accordance with the laws of the Republic of Singapore.*

190. (B) *The author verifies that the work is original, except for excerpts from copyrighted works included with proper permission.* Choices (A), (C), and (D) are contradicted by *the author verifies that the work is original, except for excerpts from copyrighted works included with proper permission.*

191. (D) *The author agrees to deliver to the publisher... supplementary instructional material, if required by the publisher.* Choice (A) is not mentioned. Choice (B) is contradicted by *two double-spaced word-processed copies.* Choice (C) is not mentioned.

192. (A) *The publisher agrees to pay author royalties... for each copy sold in Asia.* Choices (B), (C), and (D) are contradicted by *the publisher agrees to pay author royalties... for each copy sold in Asia.*

193. (A) *For beginners..., a three-night Instruction package includes...* Choices (B), (C), and (D) are contradicted by *for beginners..., a three-night Instruction package includes...*

194. (C) The Instruction package is three nights, the Eagle package is three nights, and the Hole-in-One package is five nights; therefore, they are all at least three nights. Choice (A) is incorrect because they do not all cost the same. Choice (B) is incorrect because only the Eagle package includes cart rental. Choice (D) is incorrect because only the Instruction package includes club rental.

195. (A) *During the normally slack summer months* means when business is slow. Choices (B), (C), and (D) are not mentioned.

196. (B) *During May and June, traditionally the peak months for the sale of suits...* Choices (A), (C), and (D) are contradicted by *during May and June, traditionally the peak months for the sale of suits.*

197. (C) *Your tired suit will be donated to the charity of your choice.* Choices (A), (B), and (D) are contradicted by *your tired suit will be donated to the charity of your choice.*

198. (D) *They usually fit on a desktop... hence the term* desktop. Choices (A), (B), and (C) are not mentioned.

199. (B) *Although microcomputers are the least powerful of the three types of computers, they are still more powerful than the first generation of computers.* Choices (A), (C), and (D) are not mentioned.

200. (D) *Microcomputers are popular with small businesses because they are relatively inexpensive...* Choices (A), (B), and (C) are not mentioned.

TEST
three

TEST OF ENGLISH FOR
INTERNATIONAL COMMUNICATION

General Directions

This is a test of your ability to use the English language. The total time for the test is approximately two and a half hours. It is divided into seven parts. Each part of the test begins with a set of specific directions. Be sure you understand what you are to do before you begin to work on a part.

You will find that some of the questions are harder than others, but you should try to answer every one. There is no penalty for guessing. Do not be concerned if you cannot answer all of the questions.

Do not mark your answers in this test book. **You must put all of your answers on the separate answer sheet** that you have been given. When putting your answer to a question on your answer sheet, be sure to fill in the answer space corresponding to the letter of your choice. Fill in the space so that the letter inside the oval cannot be seen, as shown in the example below.

EXAMPLE

Mr. Palmer _____ with the president last month.
(A)   meet
(B)   meeting
(C)   met
(D)   to meet

Sample Answer: (A)   (B)   ●   (D)

The sentence should read, "Mr. Palmer met with the president last month." Therefore, you should choose answer (C). Notice how this has been done in the example given.

Mark only **ONE** answer for each question. If you change your mind about an answer after you have marked it on your answer sheet, completely erase your old answer and then mark your new answer. You must mark the answer sheet carefully so that your score can be recorded accurately.

LISTENING COMPREHENSION

In this section of the test, you will have the chance to show how well you understand spoken English. There are four parts to this section, with special directions for each part.

Directions

For each question, you will see a picture in your test book and you will hear four short statements. The statements will be spoken just one time. They will not be written in your test book, so you must listen carefully to understand what the speaker says.

When you hear the four statements, look at the picture in your test book and choose the statement that best describes what you see in the picture. Then, on your answer sheet, find the number of the question and mark your answer. Look at the sample below.

EXAMPLE

Now listen to the four statements.

Example:

You will hear:
   (A)   The man is tearing the paper.
   (B)   The man is signing his name.
   (C)   The man is reading a letter.
   (D)   The man is opening an envelope.

Statement (B), "The man is signing his name," best describes what you see in the picture. Therefore, you should choose answer (B).

GO ON TO THE NEXT PAGE

4

5

6

GO ON TO THE NEXT PAGE

10

11

12

13

14

15

GO ON TO THE NEXT PAGE

16 ▶

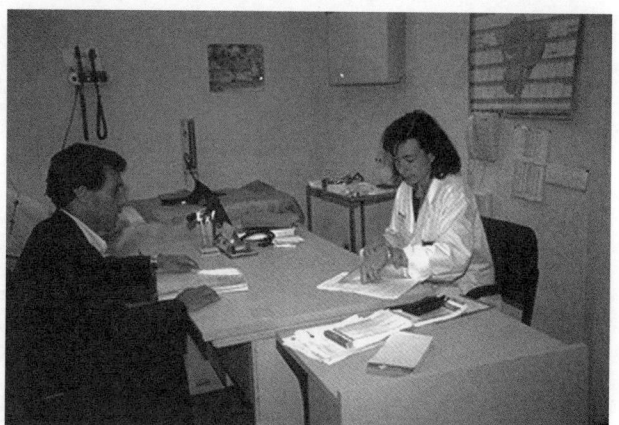

17 ▶

18 ▶

GO ON TO THE NEXT PAGE

Directions

In this part of the test, you will hear a question spoken in English, followed by three responses, also spoken in English. The question and the responses will be spoken just one time. They will not be written out for you. You must listen carefully to understand what you hear. You are to choose the best response to each question.

EXAMPLE

Now listen to a sample question.

You will hear: Good morning, John. How are you?

You will also hear: (A)   I am fine, thank you.
(B)   I am in the living room.
(C)   My name is John.

The best response to the question "How are you?" is choice (A), "I am fine, thank you." Therefore, you should choose answer (A).

21. Mark your answer on your answer sheet.

22. Mark your answer on your answer sheet.

23. Mark your answer on your answer sheet.

24. Mark your answer on your answer sheet.

25. Mark your answer on your answer sheet.

26. Mark your answer on your answer sheet.

27. Mark your answer on your answer sheet.

28. Mark your answer on your answer sheet.

29. Mark your answer on your answer sheet.

30. Mark your answer on your answer sheet.

31. Mark your answer on your answer sheet.

32. Mark your answer on your answer sheet.

33. Mark your answer on your answer sheet.

34. Mark your answer on your answer sheet.

35. Mark your answer on your answer sheet.

36. Mark your answer on your answer sheet.

37. Mark your answer on your answer sheet.

38. Mark your answer on your answer sheet.

39. Mark your answer on your answer sheet.

40. Mark your answer on your answer sheet.

41. Mark your answer on your answer sheet.

42. Mark your answer on your answer sheet.

43. Mark your answer on your answer sheet.

44. Mark your answer on your answer sheet.

45. Mark your answer on your answer sheet.

46. Mark your answer on your answer sheet.

47. Mark your answer on your answer sheet.

48. Mark your answer on your answer sheet.

49. Mark your answer on your answer sheet.

50. Mark your answer on your answer sheet.

Directions

In this part of the test, you will hear short conversations between two people. The conversations will not be written in your test book. You will hear the conversations only once; therefore, you must listen carefully.

In your test book, you will read a short question about each conversation. The question will be followed by four short answers. You are to choose the best answer to each question and mark it on your answer sheet.

51. What is the man's problem?
(A) He needs help selecting a television.
(B) He can't reach customer service.
(C) His television is not working properly.
(D) He is snowed in.

52. What will the man probably do?
(A) Go to Lisbon himself.
(B) Not send the letter express.
(C) Use the Express service.
(D) Find a quicker way to send the letter.

53. What does the woman want to know?
(A) Where the travel agency is
(B) How to get to South Street
(C) If the man cuts his own hair
(D) The name of the man's hairdresser

54. What will the woman do?
(A) Advertise in the paper.
(B) Work part-time.
(C) Take a cruise.
(D) Hire full-time workers.

55. What time is Mr. Kim's interview?
(A) 1:00
(B) 2:30
(C) 9:00
(D) 9:30

56. What is the maximum number of copies that can be made without sending the job out?
(A) 98
(B) 99
(C) 100
(D) 101

57. What is the woman's problem?
(A) She cannot reach the operator.
(B) She keeps getting a busy signal.
(C) She did not dial nine first.
(D) She did not know the country code.

58. What is important to the man?
(A) The cost of the flight
(B) The airline carrier
(C) The airline schedule
(D) The route the plane takes

59. What does the man hope?
(A) That Suzanne will be friendly.
(B) That the woman will meet Suzanne.
(C) That Suzanne will stay on the job.
(D) That a new switchboard operator will be found.

60. What does the woman learn?
(A) The driver will not take an additional passenger.
(B) They will need to pay extra.
(C) There is a flat rate to the Fairview Hotel.
(D) There will be no additional charge.

GO ON TO THE NEXT PAGE

61. What will the woman probably do the next day?
    (A) Finish the budget.
    (B) Go over the accounts.
    (C) Go sightseeing.
    (D) Get to the office by noon.

62. Why does the woman think the pizza place closed?
    (A) The service was too slow.
    (B) The chain did not research the market.
    (C) The location was not good.
    (D) The chain expanded too quickly.

63. How much would two tickets cost this weekend?
    (A) $25.00
    (B) $40.00
    (C) $50.00
    (D) $80.00

64. What is Pat Brickett's profession?
    (A) A consultant
    (B) A veterinarian
    (C) A lawyer
    (D) A linguist

65. Why will they use the televison to pay the bill?
    (A) The television is tuned to Channel 3.
    (B) It will be faster.
    (C) They won't have to pay for additional charges.
    (D) They will get only one bill.

66. Why does the state have so many toll booths?
    (A) To employ workers.
    (B) To keep drivers awake.
    (C) To slow down the traffic.
    (D) To avoid a state income tax.

67. What is the woman waiting for?
    (A) The address of her new apartment
    (B) An appointment with Debby
    (C) An e-mail address
    (D) To see the man's cards first

68. What are they discussing?
    (A) Checking in luggage
    (B) Vacationing in Cairo
    (C) Traveling together
    (D) Looking for luggage

69. Why does the woman want to speak to Linda?
    (A) Because she is the fastest worker
    (B) Because she has all the paperwork
    (C) Because she is a friend of the woman
    (D) Because she is the owner of the building

70. Why does the woman want to borrow the book?
    (A) She cannot find it in the bookstore.
    (B) She does not have the money to buy it.
    (C) She does not want to buy any more books.
    (D) She does not have a library card.

71. What are they discussing?
    (A) The local currency
    (B) Finding a bank that charges less
    (C) How many transactions they will have
    (D) What the exchange rate is

72. Why does the woman pick up her paycheck?
    (A) It is a habit.
    (B) It is simpler.
    (C) She doesn't know how to get direct deposit.
    (D) She wants to get paid on Fridays.

73. Why does the woman like where she works?
    (A) She loves being downtown.
    (B) She does not have to have a car.
    (C) She does not like the suburbs.
    (D) She can see the subway from her window.

74. What has the woman been asked to do?
    (A) Collect money for the party.
    (B) Invite Nancy's family to the party.
    (C) Organize Nancy's party.
    (D) Find a hotel for the party.

75. What is learned about the office tower?
    (A) Its rents have gone sky high.
    (B) It is being renovated.
    (C) Its location is being moved.
    (D) It has new owners.

76. Why is the man upset?
    (A) He is comfortable with the current software.
    (B) The current software does not do what he needs it to.
    (C) He thinks the new software is wrong for him.
    (D) He never gets training during work time.

77. What does the woman learn?
    (A) That it will be expensive to move to Australia.
    (B) That her moving expenses will be paid.
    (C) That she will be moving to Australia.
    (D) That the company provides a fixed amount for relocation.

78. Why would the woman use the new service?
    (A) Their rates are lower.
    (B) She does not have a car.
    (C) Her tapes would be returned on time.
    (D) They have a better selection.

79. What does the man suggest?
    (A) That they assess the projections.
    (B) That they analyze sales according to region.
    (C) That she spend a few days getting ready.
    (D) That she have an impressive presentation.

80. What are they discussing?
    (A) A tour of the plant
    (B) Her job description
    (C) The location of his office
    (D) When she will begin work

GO ON TO THE NEXT PAGE

Directions

In this part of the test, you will hear several short talks. Each will be spoken just one time. They will not be written out for you; therefore, you will have to listen carefully in order to understand and remember what is said.

In your test book, you will read two or more questions about each short talk. The questions will be followed by four answers. You are to choose the best answer to each question and mark it on your answer sheet.

81. Where is this announcement being made?
(A) In a classroom
(B) In an airport
(C) In a hospital
(D) In a theater

82. How are the doors marked?
(A) With the word *Emergency*
(B) With the word *Exit*
(C) With the word *Front*
(D) With the word *Rear*

83. What season is it now?
(A) Winter
(B) Spring
(C) Summer
(D) Fall

84. How has the weather been for the past two months?
(A) Dry
(B) Cool
(C) Rainy
(D) Hot

85. What will be reported during the day?
(A) The continued rain
(B) Tomorrow's forecast
(C) The start of thunderstorms
(D) The temperature

86. What can be said about the campaign?
(A) Four million dollars needs to be raised.
(B) The targeted amount has been raised.
(C) It relies on public funds.
(D) Funds will be collected at the luncheon.

87. What is the primary goal of the campaign?
(A) To meet institutional objectives.
(B) To increase membership.
(C) To reopen the museum.
(D) To sponsor a luncheon.

88. What is one of the purposes of the annual campaign?
(A) To renovate the garden courtyard.
(B) To institute educational programs.
(C) To add permanent collections.
(D) To sponsor luncheons.

89. Who received this letter?
(A) Hotels where guests are staying
(B) Those who had preregistered
(C) People planning to register
(D) Taxi drivers who will bring guests

90. What will probably be included in the rest of the memo?
(A) Registration costs
(B) Dates of the expo
(C) A list of the various events
(D) The number of people attending

91. How long had Jeffrey Stevens been the chief executive?
    (A) Since 1992
    (B) Two years
    (C) Ten years
    (D) Fifty years

92. What is being announced?
    (A) The Food and Drug Administration's approval of a vitamin for the U.S.
    (B) Donna Cardone's move to Brussels
    (C) The annual profits of Ever Young
    (D) The resignation of the chief executive

93. Who takes these vitamins?
    (A) Citizens of the U.S. exclusively
    (B) People over fifty
    (C) Only Europeans
    (D) Youngsters

94. What is being announced?
    (A) The purchase of an office building
    (B) The merger of two companies
    (C) The restructuring of a company
    (D) The construction of a new tower

95. How many floors are in the building?
    (A) One
    (B) Fifteen
    (C) Twenty
    (D) One hundred

96. When can tenants occupy the offices?
    (A) Immediately
    (B) After an initial inspection
    (C) Once the train station opens
    (D) This spring

97. Where are the people who are listening to this announcement?
    (A) On a bus
    (B) At a bus stop
    (C) On a commuter train
    (D) At the City Tour office

98. What were the people advised?
    (A) To be back at 1:00
    (B) To look for any Global Tours bus
    (C) To take notes
    (D) Not to leave valuables behind

99. What is the job being advertised?
    (A) Export director
    (B) Marketing coordinator
    (C) Personnel director
    (D) Travel coordinator

100. How should applicants apply for the job?
    (A) In person
    (B) By fax
    (C) By e-mail
    (D) By calling the personnel director

This is the end of the Listening Comprehension portion of the test. Turn to Part V in your test book.

GO ON TO THE NEXT PAGE

READING

In this section of the test, you will have the chance to show how well you understand written English. There are three parts to this section, with special directions for each part.

Directions

This part of the test has incomplete sentences. Four words or phrases, marked (A), (B), (C), (D), are given beneath each sentence. You are to choose the **ONE** word or phrase that best completes the sentence. Then, on your answer sheet, find the number of the question and mark your answer.

EXAMPLE

Because the equipment is very delicate, it must be handled with _____ .
(A) caring
(B) careful
(C) care
(D) carefully

The sentence should read, "Because the equipment is very delicate, it must be handled with care." Therefore, you should choose answer (C).

Now begin work on the questions.

101. _____ I am interested in accounting, I will not be attending the seminar.
(A) Because
(B) Neither
(C) Although
(D) As

102. Now that we have the new copier, it shouldn't _____ long to make all the copies.
(A) do
(B) make
(C) happen
(D) take

103. Of the two reports, the second is the _____.
(A) best
(B) better
(C) good
(D) goodly

104. Some people prefer learning a new computer program by reading the manual, while _____ prefer to play around with it.
(A) others
(B) another
(C) the others
(D) some other

105. Ms. Fujita tries to spend her lunch hour
_____.
(A) to swim
(B) going swim
(C) to go swimming
(D) swimming

106. In order to get a driver's license in _____
states, you must be at least sixteen.
(A) most of
(B) almost all of
(C) most
(D) almost of

107. We wrote the proposal entirely by _____.
(A) us
(B) ourselves
(C) our
(D) we

108. Entrepreneurs should strike the right balance
_____ advertising and selling.
(A) between
(B) both
(C) among
(D) neither

109. Alpha-Beta Corporation announced _____
clinical results for its first drug.
(A) disappointing
(B) disconnecting
(C) disagreeing
(D) disappearing

110. No one knows what the _____ result of the
marketing blitz will be.
(A) concluding
(B) remote
(C) last
(D) end

111. About five years _____, the companies
decided not to merge.
(A) before
(B) since
(C) ago
(D) past

112. The _____ author will be signing copies of
his book at the reception.
(A) sell-off
(B) bestselling
(C) sellers market
(D) packaged

113. The Tokyo Stock Exchange reported that
stocks _____.
(A) lower ended moderately today
(B) ended lower moderately today
(C) ended moderately lower today
(D) today moderately lower ended

114. Clothing sales at specialized clothing
retailers _____ in the past five years.
(A) had been risen
(B) rising
(C) are rising
(D) have risen

115. Profits indicate that the computer industry
has finally turned _____.
(A) around
(B) back
(C) forward
(D) down

116. Many companies believe that their lack of
knowledge about global markets is an
insurmountable _____.
(A) border
(B) limit
(C) barrier
(D) access

GO ON TO THE NEXT PAGE

117. Before buying a franchise, one must do a thorough job of evaluating the _____.
    (A) opponent
    (B) opinion
    (C) opportunity
    (D) opposite

118. Technology _____ constantly changing.
    (A) since it is
    (B) is
    (C) that is
    (D) will have been

119. The mortgage payments are due at the _____ of each month.
    (A) beginning
    (B) middle
    (C) twentieth
    (D) final

120. There is no _____ way to begin the preparation of a business plan.
    (A) itself
    (B) alone
    (C) only
    (D) single

121. The temperature is higher on the second floor _____ in the lobby.
    (A) by
    (B) or
    (C) than
    (D) as

122. Stationery embossed with the company logo is kept in the _____ drawer.
    (A) below
    (B) bottom
    (C) under
    (D) beneath

123. After carrying too _____ inventory for six months, the mail order company went out of business.
    (A) little
    (B) less
    (C) few
    (D) small

124. Almost _____ in the department signed up for the company picnic.
    (A) each
    (B) anyone
    (C) someone
    (D) everyone

125. No one was surprised to learn how much money the company spends _____ advertising yearly.
    (A) in
    (B) throughout
    (C) on
    (D) at

126. A retirement plan ensures one's well-being in one's _____.
    (A) oldness
    (B) old age
    (C) elderly
    (D) senile

127. I will never forget the _____ I spent in Fiji.
    (A) time
    (B) trip
    (C) travel
    (D) journey

128. Smoking _____ in this restaurant.
    (A) has no permission
    (B) will not be admitted
    (C) cannot be done
    (D) is not allowed

129. The forms _____ you need to fill out can be completed at home.
- (A) how
- (B) why
- (C) that
- (D) those

130. All of the team members are looking forward to _____ the project.
- (A) conclude
- (B) concluding
- (C) a conclusion
- (D) in conclusion

131. Ms. Freeland was hired because she is _____ in the use and teaching of word processing.
- (A) knowhow
- (B) acknowledge
- (C) knowledge
- (D) knowledgeable

132. As the price of heating oil increases, _____ does the price of electricity.
- (A) simultaneous
- (B) together
- (C) as
- (D) so

133. As is the case with most new businesses, the bakery did not make a profit in its first year of _____.
- (A) progression
- (B) operation
- (C) potential
- (D) maintenance

134. Mr. Davidson launched his first successful _____ at age fifteen, when he produced his own radio program.
- (A) profitability
- (B) venture
- (C) equity
- (D) revenue

135. The day's catch consists mostly of tuna and bluefish, with an _____ sand shark.
- (A) occasionally
- (B) on occasion
- (C) occasion
- (D) occasional

136. Ideal employers treat their employees the way they _____ would like to be treated.
- (A) themselves
- (B) selves
- (C) by themselves
- (D) to them

137. Instead of alleviating the situation, the new switchboard system turned out to be a big _____.
- (A) problematic
- (B) problematically
- (C) problem
- (D) problematical

138. While more studies are needed to _____ the findings, management will implement the recommendations immediately.
- (A) conceive
- (B) confirm
- (C) contact
- (D) conform

139. Many gold stocks posted a quarter _____.
- (A) loss
- (B) less
- (C) slow
- (D) disappointment

140. The nation's largest bank announced yesterday that it _____ all its international advertising.
- (A) consolidates
- (B) has to be consolidated
- (C) will be consolidated
- (D) would consolidate

GO ON TO THE NEXT PAGE

Directions

In this part of the test, each sentence has four words or phrases underlined. The four underlined parts of the sentence are marked (A), (B), (C), (D). You are to identify the **ONE** underlined word or phrase that should be corrected or rewritten. Then, on your answer sheet, find the number of the question and mark your answer.

EXAMPLE

All <u>employee</u> are required <u>to wear</u> their <u>identification</u> badges <u>while</u> at work.
    A   B   C   D

Choice (A), the underlined word "employee," is not correct in this sentence. The sentence should read, "All employees are required to wear their identification badges while at work." Therefore, you should choose answer (A).

Now begin work on the questions.

141. More than two <u>millions</u> dollars <u>is</u> spent
                    A   B
<u>on advertising</u> by that company <u>yearly</u>.
   C   D

142. Packages <u>are arranged</u> and labeled
               A
<u>alphabetically</u> <u>according</u> their <u>final</u>
    B   C   D
destination.

143. <u>All</u> students <u>enrolled</u> in the hotel
  A   B
administration program must <u>to complete</u>
                           C
<u>an</u> internship.
 D

144. <u>Because</u> the recorded message plays <u>so</u>
   A   B
quickly, many callers need <u>it</u> <u>repeated again</u>.
                          C   D

145. <u>Due to</u> a lack of <u>equipments</u>, the wheat crop
   A   B
in certain regions <u>is</u> <u>less than</u> expected.
               C   D

146. Public telephones <u>are located</u> <u>on</u> the <u>seventh</u>
                    A   B   C
floor, in the basement, and <u>on</u> the lobby.
                            D

147. Alike publicly-held companies, private firms
‎ ‎ ‎ ‎ ‎ A ‎ ‎ ‎ B
can make decisions without a majority
‎ ‎ ‎ C ‎ ‎ ‎ ‎ ‎ D
consensus.

148. Computer knowledge has become more
‎ ‎ ‎ ‎ ‎ ‎ ‎ ‎ ‎ ‎ ‎ ‎ ‎ ‎ ‎ ‎ A
commoner even among very young children.
‎ ‎ ‎ B ‎ ‎ ‎ ‎ ‎ ‎ C ‎ ‎ ‎ ‎ ‎ ‎ ‎ ‎ ‎ ‎ D

149. Alaska's income comes from gas and oil
‎ ‎ ‎ ‎ ‎ ‎ ‎ ‎ ‎ ‎ ‎ ‎ ‎ A ‎ ‎ ‎ B
production, enabling the state reducing
‎ ‎ ‎ ‎ ‎ ‎ ‎ ‎ ‎ ‎ C ‎ ‎ ‎ ‎ ‎ ‎ ‎ ‎ ‎ ‎ D
taxes.

150. Our new long-distance phone service it is
‎ ‎ ‎ A ‎ ‎ ‎ ‎ ‎ ‎ ‎ ‎ ‎ ‎ ‎ ‎ ‎ ‎ ‎ ‎ ‎ ‎ ‎ B
cheaper and more reliable than its
‎ ‎ ‎ ‎ ‎ ‎ ‎ ‎ ‎ ‎ C ‎ ‎ ‎ ‎ ‎ D
competitors.

151. Mrs. Wong introduced his replacement to all
‎ ‎ ‎ ‎ ‎ ‎ ‎ ‎ A ‎ ‎ ‎ ‎ B
the secretarial staff before leaving on Friday.
‎ ‎ ‎ ‎ ‎ C ‎ ‎ ‎ ‎ ‎ ‎ ‎ ‎ ‎ ‎ ‎ ‎ ‎ ‎ ‎ D

152. The running shoe store in the mall

is looking for salespersons who are
‎ ‎ ‎ A ‎ ‎ ‎ ‎ ‎ ‎ ‎ ‎ ‎ ‎ ‎ ‎ B
very knowledge about their products.
‎ C ‎ ‎ ‎ D

153. Not employee is permitted to use the copy
‎ ‎ ‎ A ‎ ‎ ‎ ‎ ‎ B
machine for personal use.
‎ ‎ ‎ ‎ ‎ ‎ ‎ C ‎ ‎ ‎ ‎ ‎ D

154. A letter of credit permits an individual or a

business drawing up to a stated amount of
‎ ‎ ‎ ‎ ‎ ‎ ‎ A ‎ ‎ ‎ ‎ ‎ ‎ ‎ B ‎ ‎ ‎ C
money from that bank.
‎ ‎ ‎ ‎ ‎ D

155. After meeting with local citizens and
‎ ‎ ‎ A
investors, the architecture designed a
‎ ‎ ‎ B ‎ ‎ ‎ ‎ ‎ ‎ C
shopping center which was pleasing to all.
‎ ‎ ‎ ‎ ‎ ‎ ‎ ‎ ‎ ‎ ‎ ‎ ‎ D

156. If you are not satisfied since two weeks,
‎ ‎ ‎ ‎ ‎ A ‎ ‎ ‎ ‎ ‎ ‎ B
return the television in its original carton for
‎ ‎ ‎ ‎ ‎ ‎ ‎ ‎ ‎ ‎ ‎ ‎ ‎ C
a full refund.
‎ ‎ D

157. A company's cash flow is more important
‎ ‎ ‎ ‎ ‎ ‎ ‎ ‎ ‎ ‎ ‎ ‎ ‎ A ‎ ‎ ‎ B
than either the income statement nor the
‎ C ‎ ‎ ‎ ‎ ‎ ‎ ‎ ‎ ‎ ‎ ‎ ‎ ‎ ‎ D
balance sheet.

158. Although the major of patients seen by
‎ ‎ ‎ ‎ ‎ ‎ ‎ A ‎ ‎ ‎ ‎ ‎ ‎ B
Dr. Joyce are referred by friends,
‎ ‎ ‎ ‎ ‎ C
on occasion a new patient finds Dr. Joyce's
‎ ‎ ‎ D
name in the phonebook.

159. This software enables users to access
‎ ‎ ‎ ‎ ‎ ‎ ‎ ‎ A ‎ ‎ ‎ ‎ ‎ ‎ ‎ ‎ B
collections of logic related data.
‎ ‎ ‎ ‎ ‎ ‎ ‎ C ‎ ‎ ‎ ‎ D

160. The conclusion of the investigating team is
‎ ‎ ‎ ‎ ‎ ‎ ‎ ‎ ‎ ‎ ‎ ‎ ‎ ‎ ‎ ‎ A
that workers with flexible schedules are
‎ ‎ ‎ ‎ ‎ ‎ ‎ ‎ ‎ ‎ ‎ B
happier than others workers.
‎ ‎ ‎ ‎ C ‎ ‎ ‎ D

GO ON TO THE NEXT PAGE

Part vii

Directions

The questions in this part of the test are based on a variety of reading material, such as notices, letters, newspapers and magazine articles, and advertisements. You are to choose the **ONE** best answer, (A), (B), (C), or (D), to each question. Then, on your answer sheet, find the number of the question and mark your answer. Answer all questions following a passage on the basis of what is **stated** or **implied** in that passage.

EXAMPLE

Read the following example.

> The Museum of Technology is designed for people to experience science at work. Visitors are encouraged to use, test, and handle the objects on display. Special demonstrations are scheduled for the first and second Wednesdays of each month at 1:30 p.m. Open Tuesday-Friday, 2:30-4:30 p.m., Saturday 11:00 a.m. -4:30 p.m., and Sunday 1:00-4:30 p.m.

When during the month can visitors see special demonstrations?
(A)   Every weekend
(B)   The first two Wednesdays
(C)   One afternoon a week
(D)   Every other Wednesday

The passage says that the demonstrations are scheduled on the first and second Wednesdays of the month. Therefore, you should choose answer (B).

Now begin work on the questions.

When Electricom And Gasco Had The Bright Idea To Become Partners, It Wasn't A Light Bulb That Went On

The idea was simple. Electricom, a leader in electricity with more expertise than anyone in the field, wanted a partner in natural gas. One company's name kept coming up. Gasco, one of the country's largest natural gas marketers, had a history of dedication to its customers and had consistently been rated #1 in customer satisfaction.

Electricom feels that this partnership with Gasco gives the company a competitive edge. For one thing, it marks the first time Electricom can sell natural gas. Secondly, Electricom can now expand its reach beyond its Michigan base.

161. What is the main purpose of this announcement?
(A) To analyze the natural gas market
(B) To announce a joint venture
(C) To investigate electrical companies
(D) To encourage applicants

162. What was Electricom seeking?
(A) A simpler product
(B) A marketing strategy
(C) A natural gas partner
(D) A better light bulb

163. Which of the following is true about Electricom?
(A) It is known for selling natural gas.
(B) It is seeking additional partners.
(C) It is generally ranked first in customer satisfaction.
(D) It is located in Michigan.

GO ON TO THE NEXT PAGE

Questions 164–166 refer to the following advertisement.

The First Healthy Toothpaste.
No saccharin. No preservatives. No dyes.

All major brands of toothpaste contain saccharin and preservatives. Many contain dyes. These ingredients contribute nothing to good oral hygiene.

Dan's of Martha's Vineyard is committed to products made with safe and effective natural ingredients. We use natural calcium to make your teeth really clean, fluoride from natural fluorspar to help prevent cavities, and natural spearmint oil to freshen your entire mouth with a clean tingle.

Natural ingredients make the difference. Try our healthy approach to oral care as well as any of our other various beauty products. Then write us a note to let us know how you feel.

Dan and Joan Roberts ● 1621 Indian Valley Way
Martha's Vineyard ● Massachusetts

164. Which of the following does Dan's contain?
- (A) Calcium
- (B) Saccharin
- (C) Dyes
- (D) Preservatives

165. What other item would Dan's likely produce?
- (A) Stationery
- (B) Paintbrushes
- (C) Shampoo
- (D) Life preservers

166. Which of the following does Dan's NOT claim?
- (A) Clean teeth
- (B) Low prices
- (C) Cavity prevention
- (D) Freshened mouths

Questions 167–169 refer to the following offer.

Become a Village Member and Get the Reduced Admission Price of $4.50 for All Films

Belong to an Independent Movie House Showing Independent Films for Independent Eyes

Other great membership benefits include:

- 2 for 1 video rentals at VideoStar
- 10% discount at City CDs
- 25% discount at Bay Booksellers
- Free coffee with any bakery purchase at Casual Cup Coffee House

Please fill out this coupon immediately.

Level of Membership:

[ ] Silver $50.
[ ] Gold $100.
[ ] Platinum $500.
[ ] This is a new membership.
[ ] This is a straight donation.
[ ] This is a renewal.
[ ] My company will match my payment.

Form of Payment

[ ] Check
[ ] Cash

167. Which of the following is an additional benefit of membership?
(A) CDs reduced by one quarter
(B) Free baked goods
(C) Theater rentals
(D) Book discounts

168. According to the advertisement, what is an option?
(A) Donating money
(B) Paying in installments
(C) Using a credit card
(D) Reduced film prices without becoming a member

169. If a person joins as a Gold Member and her firm matches her gift, how much will Village receive?
(A) $100
(B) $150
(C) $200
(D) $400

GO ON TO THE NEXT PAGE

The Federal Trade Commission (FTC) has changed the care symbols required to print on clothing labels. Much like the new Federal Communication Commission (FCC) television rating codes, the new symbols, designed to be simple, will no doubt cause senseless confusion as well as heartbreaking shrinkage for the next couple of years.

To avoid gambling with the longevity of precious garments, you can request the commission's jazzy new brochure: *Closet Cues: Care Labels and Your Clothes.* Just call the Consumer Response Center at the FTC, telephone **(203) 536-2222**, or check the FTC Consumerline at **www.ftc.gov.org.**

170. To whom is this notice most likely addressed?
(A) Tailors and seamstresses
(B) Anyone who washes clothes
(C) Members of the FTC
(D) Television viewers

171. What does the notice say is likely to occur?
(A) It will take several years to create symbols.
(B) The FTC will use the FCC symbols.
(C) People will be delighted with the simple codes.
(D) Garments will not be washed as they should.

172. What can be said about the new brochure?
(A) It is expensive.
(B) It is printed by the FCC.
(C) It is flashy.
(D) It will take several years to be printed.

Think that those airplane phones are just for corporate executives? Throughout the summer, air travelers can take advantage of ABC Airfone's summer savings. Between now and September 1, passengers can dial *995 while in flight to purchase ten minutes of domestic calls for only $9.95, an average of 99 cents per minute. The normal charge for a domestic call is $2.99 per connection, plus $3.28 per minute or fraction thereof — a bit steep for some wallets. All you need is a major credit card.

173. When is the promotion going to take place?
(A) Until the end of the summer
(B) Two summers in a row
(C) From this summer until next summer
(D) During the month of September

174. Where can a passenger flying in the U.S. call using this plan?
(A) From the U.S. to Japan
(B) Anywhere in the U.S.
(C) Only to one's home number
(D) To other in-flight passengers

175. What is the average cost of a call that lasts three minutes when this plan is not in effect?
(A) $2.97
(B) $2.99
(C) $9.84
(D) $12.83

GO ON TO THE NEXT PAGE

Questions 176–178 refer to the following news article.

The British pound tumbled yesterday after the Bank of England signaled that British interest rates had risen high enough. The pound fell to a ten-month low against the dollar and a one-month low against the German mark. The dollar fell as well against most major currencies, posting its first loss against the mark after a string of gains which had brought it to an eight-year high.

The British central bank raised its official interest rate to 7 percent from 6.75 percent, its fourth consecutive monthly increase. At the same time the bank released a statement saying it had no immediate plans for future rate increases, which prompted heavy sales of pounds.

Against the Japanese yen, the dollar fell in part on expectations that reports will show Japan's current account surplus — the broadest measure of trade — had widened sharply in June. The dollar settled at 118.45 yen, down from 118.68 yen on Wednesday.

176. Which of the following did NOT happen yesterday?
(A) The British pound fell against most leading currencies.
(B) The dollar fell against the mark.
(C) The mark reached an eight-year high against the dollar.
(D) The dollar fell against the Japanese yen.

177. Why was there heavy selling of the British pound?
(A) Interest rates in Britain had risen for four consecutive months.
(B) The dollar fell against the German mark.
(C) Interest rates will not increase in the near future.
(D) The official interest rate is now 7%.

178. What explains the dollar falling in Japan?
(A) Its fall against the German mark.
(B) The heavy selling of pounds.
(C) The decrease in trade with Japan.
(D) The reports of Japan's trade surplus.

Questions 179–182 refer to the following poll.

Living Better Than Your Parents Did at Your Age?

Economists, political candidates, and newspaper reporters have focused on a downward slope in the national standard of living ever since the prosperous 1960's. Surprisingly, people persist in telling pollsters that they feel they're doing just fine.

In a nationwide survey conducted last week by a marketing research firm, respondents were asked: **Are you living better than your parents did at your age?**

Last year 71 percent said they are living better than their parents, whereas respondents this year who said that their standard of living is better than their parents' rose to 82 percent. Of those who said they're not doing better than their parents, a majority (56 percent) said they are faring as well as their folks did. Respondents in the supposedly dispirited 18- to 24-year-old age group were even more likely than the sample as a whole to say their standard of living exceeds that of their parents at the same age.

179. Who conducted the survey?
- (A) A research team
- (B) Economists
- (C) Political candidates
- (D) Newspaper editors

180. What percent of respondents this year said they were doing worse than their parents?
- (A) Eighteen
- (B) Twenty-nine
- (C) Forty-four
- (D) Fifty-six

181. What were the responses of eighteen- to twenty-four-year-olds expected to be?
- (A) More likely to say their standard exceeds their parents'
- (B) More positive than other groups
- (C) More negative than other groups
- (D) No different from other age groups'

182. What did the survey reveal?
- (A) The older the respondent, the better he/she felt.
- (B) People agree that the standard of living was higher in the sixties.
- (C) Economists were correct in their predictions.
- (D) Increasingly, people think they are living better than their parents did.

GO ON TO THE NEXT PAGE

The World Film Festival
January 22-February 5

You can bet the stars, as well as the directors, producers, writers, and fans of cinema will be out. After all, the festival is recognized not only as one of the most important cultural events in Canada, but also as the largest publicly attended film festival in the western world. Last year, close to 350,000 film fans attended 670 screenings of 400 films from 63 countries around the world.

This year's festival promises to be even bigger and better.

183. Where is the festival being held?
  (A) All over the world
  (B) In sixty-three countries
  (C) In Canada
  (D) Throughout the western world

184. When the notice says "the stars will be out," it means
  (A) the festival will be held at night
  (B) movie stars will attend
  (C) the screenings will be outdoors
  (D) it won't be raining

185. Which of the following is true?
  (A) Some films are shown more than once.
  (B) People from sixty-three different countries were in attendance last year.
  (C) Films are produced only in western countries.
  (D) The festival is an important occasion on which to shoot films.

**If you think the buildings are big
in New York,
wait until you see the size of
a Manhattan East Suite.**

At Manhattan East Suite Hotels, you'll experience one of New York's greatest luxuries. Space. You'll stay in a large, relaxing apartment-sized suite. All suites have a kitchen and the full-service business amenities you expect — such as in-room faxes — all for the price of an ordinary hotel room. With nine hotels to choose from, you're sure to find one close to where you want to be. For reservations or a brochure, call your travel agent or 1-800-BE-LARGE, Extension 57.

186. To whom is the advertisement primarily addressed?
(A) Cooks
(B) Apartment hunters
(C) Business travelers
(D) Tourists

187. How are these suites similar to regular hotel rooms?
(A) Both include kitchens.
(B) They are the same size.
(C) Both have in-room fax machines.
(D) They cost the same.

188. What is true about the Manhattan East Suites?
(A) They look like ordinary hotel rooms.
(B) There are nine hotels with these types of rooms.
(C) Rooms must be booked by a travel agent.
(D) Most of the guests live in the suites permanently.

GO ON TO THE NEXT PAGE

Questions 189–192 refer to the following notice.

FRANKFURT-BASED BRITISH RETAILER WANTS TO ESTABLISH BRANCHES IN THE U.S. FOR GERMAN-BUILT STYLISH OFFICE FURNITURE.

IDEAL LOCATIONS INCLUDE ARIZONA, CALIFORNIA, AND TEXAS, BUT WILL CONSIDER FLORIDA AND THE NORTHEAST.

PREFER TO BUY EXISTING BUILDING, BUT WILL LOOK AT LEASE OPTIONS AND FEASIBILITY OF NEW CONSTRUCTION.

189. What does this retailer wish to do?
(A) To open branch outlets in the U.S.
(B) To make furniture in the U.S.
(C) To move his headquarters to the U.S.
(D) To find a U.S. partner for his operation

190. What is the retailer selling?
(A) Real estate
(B) Clothes
(C) Furniture
(D) Construction equipment

191. Which location is most desirable?
(A) Florida
(B) New York
(C) Alabama
(D) Texas

192. What kind of arrangement is most preferable?
(A) Renting a store
(B) Purchasing a building
(C) Constructing a new plant
(D) Buying an empty site

Questions 193–196 refer to the following article.

The decade of the 1980's brought a global boom in franchising. The number of U.S.-operated franchises abroad doubled to more than 40,000.

From Europe to Asia to Africa, U.S. franchisers have found receptive markets and vast opportunities to export their style of business. Successful franchises can be found on the streets of Cairo, Paris, or Moscow. Unlike businesses seeking only to market U.S. products or to build U.S.-owned plants, franchises are thriving globally because they offer opportunities for local entrepreneurs within a foreign market. Especially appealing to those entrepreneurs is the opportunity to master U.S. business methods and technology.

Global franchising is, of course, a two-way street. Today, more and more foreign franchisers are looking for franchise opportunities in the United States. Canadian franchisers enjoy the largest presence in the U.S., followed by British and Japanese franchisers. In the 1990's the boom in franchise expansion continues.

193. About how many U.S.-operated franchises were operating abroad before the 1980's?
- (A) 4,000
- (B) 20,000
- (C) 40,000
- (D) 80,000

194. Which of the following is NOT mentioned as a reason why U.S. franchisers have found success abroad?
- (A) Cheaper locations
- (B) Welcoming markets
- (C) Numerous opportunities
- (D) Eager local entrepreneurs

195. According to the article, why is global franchising a "two-way street?"
- (A) Because U.S. investors must pay taxes abroad.
- (B) Because U.S. franchisers find local investors to be partners.
- (C) Because U.S. owners enjoy teaching U.S. business methods.
- (D) Because foreign franchisers are opening franchises in the U.S.

196. Which country has the largest number of franchises in the U.S.?
- (A) Britain
- (B) Egypt
- (C) Canada
- (D) Japan

GO ON TO THE NEXT PAGE

Questions 197–200 refer to the following report.

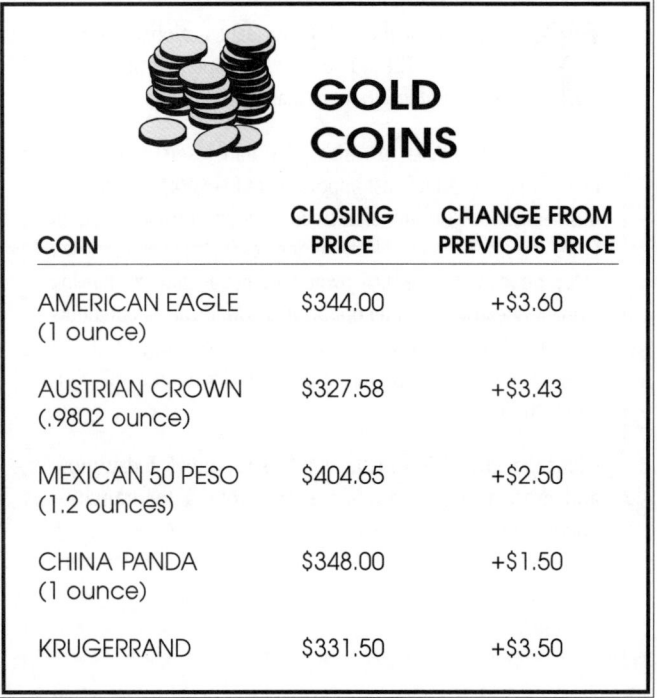

GOLD COINS

COIN	CLOSING PRICE	CHANGE FROM PREVIOUS PRICE
AMERICAN EAGLE (1 ounce)	$344.00	+$3.60
AUSTRIAN CROWN (.9802 ounce)	$327.58	+$3.43
MEXICAN 50 PESO (1.2 ounces)	$404.65	+$2.50
CHINA PANDA (1 ounce)	$348.00	+$1.50
KRUGERRAND	$331.50	+$3.50

197. Which coin's price increased the most from its previous price?
(A) The Krugerrand
(B) The American Eagle
(C) The Austrian Crown
(D) The Mexican 50 Peso

198. What was the Krugerrand's previous price?
(A) $328.00
(B) $333.00
(C) $330.00
(D) $335.00

199. Which of the following is NOT a difference among the coins?
(A) The type of metal
(B) The weight
(C) The country of origin
(D) The closing price

200. What is the price per ounce of a China Panda coin today?
(A) $3.48
(B) $34.80
(C) $346.50
(D) $348.00

Part 1

Sample Item
M: (A) The man is tearing the paper.
(B) The man is signing his name.
(C) The man is reading a letter.
(D) The man is opening an envelope.

1. *M1:* (A) The meal is being served.
(B) The waiter is placing the dishes on the table.
(C) The people are waiting to order.
(D) The customer has left the money on the table.

2. *M2:* (A) The man is getting out of the car.
(B) The man in the car is waiting for the light to change.
(C) Several people are getting into the car.
(D) The man is rolling down his car windows.

3. *F:* (A) The officers are directing traffic.
(B) The motorcycles are driving down the street.
(C) Several police officers are standing by their motorcycles.
(D) The police officers are lined up on their motorcycles.

4. *M2:* (A) The woman is folding the clothes.
(B) The woman is crossing the street.
(C) The woman is crossing the room.
(D) The woman has folded her arms.

5. *M1:* (A) The young girl is feeding her baby sister.
(B) The baby is sitting alone on the chair.
(C) The baby is sitting on the woman's lap.
(D) The young girl is playing with the baby.

6. *F:* (A) The boy is changing the tire.
(B) The boy is sledding on the tire.
(C) The boy has a flat tire.
(D) The boy is rolling the tire down the hill.

7. *M2:* (A) The flagpoles are being assembled.
(B) The flags are flying at half-mast.
(C) The flags are flying at the same height.
(D) The flagpoles are different heights.

8. *M1:* (A) The tennis ball is in motion.
(B) The tennis ball is caught in the net.
(C) The woman is choosing a partner for the tennis match.
(D) The woman is going to hit the ball with her bat.

9. *F:* (A) A bridge leads to the building.
(B) The building is built on a bridge.
(C) The bridge has been raised to let a boat pass underneath.
(D) A bridge is being built around the building.

10. *M2:* (A) The bus is passing the other cars on the street.
(B) The bus has pulled to the side of the road.
(C) The passengers are getting on the bus.
(D) The bus driver is exiting the bus.

11. *M1:* (A) The farmers are picking fruit from the trees.
(B) The farmers are driving tractors through the field.
(C) The farmers are leaving the field.
(D) The farmers are planting in the field.

12. *F:* (A) The officer is towing the car.
(B) The officer is parking the car.
(C) The officer is writing a ticket.
(D) The officer is writing on the car.

13. *M2:* (A) One man is packaging the loaves of breads.
(B) One man is working at a machine.
(C) Both men are working at a table.
(D) Both workers are pouring ingredients into the machine.

14. *M1:* (A) One car is following along behind the other.
(B) The cars are parked next to the building.
(C) The cars are driving off in opposite directions.
(D) The cars are driving side by side.

15. *F:* (A) Both men are sitting in the park.
(B) The businessmen are posing by a sculpture.
(C) The men are standing next to a sculpture.
(D) An artist is making a sculpture of the men.

16. *M2:* (A) The man is working on the computer.
(B) The man's feet are under the desk.
(C) The man has his feet up on the desk.
(D) The man is delivering the newspaper.

17. *M1:* (A) The patient is getting onto the examining table.
(B) The doctor is checking the patient's temperature.
(C) The doctor and patient are standing in the examining room.
(D) The doctor is sitting across from the patient.

18. *F:* (A) The man is handing a sheet of paper to the woman.
(B) The woman is whispering a message to the man.
(C) The woman is drawing a diagram on the paper for the man.
(D) The woman is conducting a survey on the street.

19. *M2:* (A) The man is ringing a bell in the street.
(B) The man is carrying bells in both hands.
(C) The man is swinging the bell over his head.
(D) The man is ringing a doorbell.

20. *M1:* (A) The woman is showing the man some travel brochures.
(B) The man and woman are hanging brochures on the wall.
(C) The man is turning the pages of the brochure.
(D) The woman is taking brochures down from the shelf.

Part
ii

Sample Question

W: Good morning, John. How are you?
M: (A) I am fine, thank you.
M: (B) I am in the living room.
M: (C) My name is John.

21. W: You've handed in the final draft, haven't you?
M: (A) Yes. It's cold in here.
M: (B) I have to proofread it again.
M: (C) No. I went to the playoffs last week.

22. M: Don't you ever wish you had taken the other job offer?
W: (A) I must have sent in the form.
W: (B) I try not to think about it.
W: (C) Tell him I'll see him later.

23. W: Have you lost weight?
M: (A) No. It must be my new hairstyle.
M: (B) Yes, I do.
M: (C) I have a small suitcase.

24. M: Are you hiring in the design department?
W: (A) We're looking for two replacements.
W: (B) The windows should be lower.
W: (C) The decorator chose the furniture.

25. W: How long have you worked in Singapore?
M: (A) The weather is wonderful.
M: (B) Seven weeks ago.
M: (C) Just about six months.

26. M: How often do you check your e-mail?
W: (A) No, I don't.
W: (B) For six months.
W: (C) Every morning.

27. M: Do I have to exchange my ticket at the airport?
W: (A) No. These are train tickets.
W: (B) Actually, you can do it by phone.
W: (C) I recommend taking a taxi.

28. W: Who's in charge of office supplies?
M: (A) I'll pay for them later.
M: (B) We just got a new copier.
M: (C) It's Gloria on the first floor.

29. M: Is there a gas station open at this hour?
W: (A) There's one on Second Avenue.
W: (B) Before 10:00 p.m.
W: (C) They all change tires.

30. W: Who paid for your relocation expenses?
M: (A) The apartment they found is too small.
M: (B) Thank goodness the company did.
M: (C) Because we're moving to Berlin.

31. M: What time is the conference call?
W: (A) In the Smith Room.
W: (B) At noon on the dot.
W: (C) Mr. Johnson asked to have one.

32. W: Would you rather drive or go by bus?
M: (A) Either way is fine.
M: (B) You need tokens for the subway.
M: (C) I'll take both.

33. M: What did you think of the president's memo?
W: (A) All deliveries are at 5:00.
W: (B) I thought it was today.
W: (C) I'm not sure what the point was.

34. M: That's the Federal Reserve Bank, right?
W: (A) I'm pretty sure it is.
W: (B) No, I use a local bank.
W: (C) Yes, I left my money in the room.

35. W: Who should get a copy of this letter?
M: (A) I put it in the mailbox.
M: (B) Everyone who was at the meeting.
M: (C) The stamp machine is broken.

36. M: How did you decide to start manufacturing abroad?
W: (A) We ship the goods.
W: (B) Yes, it was a timely decision.
W: (C) It costs less.

37. M: Have you ever played tennis on grass courts?
W: (A) My serve is getting better.
W: (B) No, but I'd like to try.
W: (C) The basketball court has plenty of seating.

38. W: Where is your boss spending his winter vacation?
M: (A) It's too cold in January.
M: (B) He's planning to ski in the Alps.
M: (C) About $1,000 a week.

39. M: How do you know who to tip in this country?
W: (A) I check my guidebook.
W: (B) About 15 or 20 percent.
W: (C) There are lots of tourists.

40. W: Could we stay in our room after checkout?
M: (A) Check out is at one.
M: (B) No, cancellations must be made forty-eight hours in advance.
M: (C) We'll have to charge you for another day.

41. M: Where is Joe's farewell party?
W: (A) When we went for lunch.
W: (B) At the new restaurant around the corner.
W: (C) Not until yesterday.

42. W: Why not ask Bill for a recommendation?
M: (A) What a good idea.
M: (B) This Friday before 5:00.
M: (C) I have to pay the electric bill by the thirtieth.

43. M: What accounts for this product's popularity?
W: (A) During the sales promotion.
W: (B) It's practical yet cheap.
W: (C) The product manager is late.

44. W: Who will answer the phone while Jane's out sick?
M: (A) It was a wrong number.
M: (B) If I'm not too busy, I can handle it.
M: (C) She's in the hospital.

45. **M:** *Do you take credit cards?*
    W: (A) I take credit for the increase in sales.
    W: (B) She works in the credit department.
    W: (C) No, cash only.

46. **W:** *Can I get you some coffee?*
    M: (A) Yes, with two sugars.
    M: (B) Yes, I get it.
    M: (C) No, it's cold in here.

47. **M:** *Do you think we can wrap up by this afternoon?*
    W: (A) I can wrap the gift at home.
    W: (B) With a little luck.
    W: (C) The wrapping paper is upstairs.

48. **W:** *How do I submit a claim?*
    M: (A) Are you sure it's yours?
    M: (B) No, you don't.
    M: (C) Make sure you have all the receipts.

49. **M:** *Why don't you move to Jason's old office?*
    W: (A) Third room down the hall.
    W: (B) It's bigger, but I want one with a window.
    W: (C) He got a promotion.

50. **W:** *Is everyone always so helpful around here?*
    M: (A) Yes, it's a great place to work.
    M: (B) Can I help you?
    M: (C) Yes, there's a hotel nearby.

51. W: Customer service.
    M: Yes. Can I help you?
    W: I don't know what's wrong with my television. Sometimes the picture is fine, and sometimes all I get is snow.

52. M: How much would it cost to send this letter express to Lisbon?
    W: That'll be twenty-five dollars.
    M: Twenty-five dollars? What's the next quickest way?

53. W: Where do you get your hair cut?
    M: Do you know that place next to the travel agency on South Street?
    W: Sure. Who does your hair there?

54. W: Do you think we should hire some part-time workers?
    M: We'd better, if we want to ship out all the orders by the end of the month.
    W: I'll put an ad in this weekend's paper.

55. W: Did you say Mr. Kim was coming in for the interview at 9:00?
    M: Did I say nine? I meant 9:30.
    W: I'm glad I asked one more time.

56. W: Did you get the memo about the new copying procedures?
    M: What did it say? That anything over one hundred copies has to be sent out?
    W: I'm lucky I only needed to make ninety-nine copies this morning. I need them for a meeting after lunch.

57. W: Operator, I'm trying to make an international call, and I can't get through.
    M: Did you dial nine, zero, zero, and the country code?
    W: Oh. I didn't know I had to dial nine.

58. M: Can you check the schedule for flights from Miami to San Jose, Costa Rica?
    W: Do you prefer any particular airline?
    M: No, but the fare is important to me.

59. M: Have you met the new switchboard operator?
    W: Oh, you mean Suzanne? She seems really friendly.
    M: I sure hope she stays longer than the last two.

60. W: Is there an additional charge if we share a cab?
    M: Not if you're going to the same place.
    W: Great. Take us to the Fairview Hotel, please.

61. W: I hope I'll have some time for sightseeing while I'm here this time.
    M: We should finish going over the accounts today, so we can start the budget tomorrow in the afternoon sometime.
    W: Fabulous. I've been in this city five times and have only seen this office complex!

62. W: I was sad to see the pizza place in the square close.
    M: You know, that was the sixth one the chain opened in the city this year.
    W: I guess some market researcher told them the demand was there, but it's too bad they didn't go a little slower.

63. M: The show at the Colonial has a special this weekend — four seats in the balcony for only eighty dollars.
    W: So would three tickets cost sixty dollars?
    M: No, for fewer than four, you pay the regular price of twenty-five dollars each.

64. W: Do you know why Pat Brickett resigned?
    M: I heard she's starting her own consulting firm.
    W: If she takes all of our clients with her, she'll be the talk of the town.

65. M: Remember they told us at check-in that we could pay the hotel bill using Channel 3 on the television?
    W: Right. Any charges we make afterwards will show up on a separate bill.
    M: It's such a good idea. Did you see how long the lines were?

66. W: I hate driving through this state. There are so many toll booths.
    M: They slow up traffic, and they're dangerous.
    W: Supposedly they use the revenue to avoid having a state income tax.

67. M: You can leave all your information with Debby, and she'll have business cards made up for you.
W: I'm just waiting until I get my new e-mail address.
M: Look at my cards. Don't they look great?

68. M: Are you going to check in your bag or take it on the plane?
W: Ever since I lost my suitcase in Cairo, I take it on the plane.
M: Then I will too, so we won't have to wait when we land.

69. W: Can you get the bank on the phone? I have to make some changes to the purchase and sales agreement.
M: Is it Linda who's working on it?
W: Yeah. Make sure it's Linda. Otherwise, it'll take someone new an hour just to find all the paperwork.

70. W: Can I read that book when you're finished? My name has been on the waiting list at the library for three months.
M: Sure, I should be done with it by tomorrow. There's no sense in buying it.
W: I try not to buy books if I can get them out of the library.

71. W: I'm not sure how much local currency to buy.
M: I know what you mean. Either I buy too much, or I don't buy enough.
W: Yeah, and the bank charges ten percent for every transaction.

72. M: Do you have your paycheck deposited directly into your account?
W: I know I should, but I've been picking it up every Friday for years and never got around to changing it.
M: I hear it's really simple to set up. Do you want to come with me?

73. W: Have you heard anything else about the proposed move?
M: I love working downtown. I'd hate to relocate to the suburbs.
W: It's been great having a subway nearby. If we move, I'd have to buy a car.

74. W: Guess who's in charge of organizing Nancy's engagement party. Me.
M: Oh, I'll help you. Let's make it really special. Nancy has no family around here.
W: Mr. Williams said he had budgeted enough money for us to have it at the Drake Hotel.

75. W: Finally the office tower has some new owners.
M: If that place gets fixed up, the rents could be sky high.
W: And look at the location!

76. M: Every time I learn a new software program, the department decides on another one.
W: Supposedly this time we're going to get training during work hours.
M: I don't know what's wrong with the one we have now. It does everything I need.

77. W: Will the company pay all of my relocation expenses?
M: Of course. The personnel director has a chart with the amount allocated. It depends on where you're being assigned.
W: That's great news. It's going to cost a fortune to move to Australia.

78. M: Have you tried the video rental service that delivers and picks up tapes?
W: I'm definitely going to use it. I had stopped renting after I forgot to return a tape and was charged twenty-five dollars.
M: You could have bought your own for that amount!

79. W: I've been invited to present our proposal to the mid-management group.
M: Bring color graphics and detailed handouts with sales projections according to region.
W: I know it's going to take me days to get everything ready.

80. M: Will I receive a written job description before I begin work on Monday?
W: Of course. I'll make sure you have one before you leave today.
M: Thanks. I should be done with the tour of the plant at 4:00, and I'll stop by your office then.

Questions 81 and 82 refer to the following announcement:
W: In case of an emergency, please exit calmly through the doors marked *exit*. There are doors in front of the theater as well as in the rear.

Questions 83–85 are based on the following weather report:
M1: Although these days should be the dog days of summer, temperatures will remain unseasonably cool throughout the week. There is a chance of light rain beginning this afternoon or evening, which could be accompanied by thunderstorms. Unfortunately, this slight amount of precipitation will not end our two-month drought, but the grass, flowers, and crops will welcome any nourishment. We will update you on the status of the thunderstorms throughout the day.

Questions 86–88 refer to the following speech:
M2: I'd like to interrupt the luncheon for just a few moments to announce that the museum's annual campaign has reached its goal of four million dollars. This significant accomplishment for a privately funded museum is a clear indication of the strong support of our membership. While fund-raising campaigns are, first and foremost, about raising money, they are also about meeting institutional objectives. The chief goals of this campaign are to preserve our great permanent collections, to improve our community educational programs, and to restore and reopen our garden courtyard after a thirteen-year hiatus.

W: Thank you for preregistering for the Computerworld Expo, which will run from Monday, September first through Friday, September fifth at the Bayside Expo and World Trade Center. More than fifty thousand people are expected to attend, so here's what you need to know.

M2: Ever Young Pharmaceuticals, International, announced yesterday that Jeffrey Stevens, its chief executive since the company's inception a decade ago, had resigned. The resignation took effect immediately. Ever Young, which is based in Brussels, said that Donna Cardone, its president and chief operating officer for the past two years, would oversee the company's operations until a successor for Mr. Stevens was found. Ever Young, one of the world's largest manufacturers of vitamins for those over fifty, has had increasingly profitable years since 1992 when the United States Food and Drug Administration okayed its sale in the U.S.

M1: M.A.S. Realty Management Corporation and Michaelson Limited Partners are pleased to announce the acquisition of 100 Church Street in Center City. This 615,000 square foot Class A Office Tower is conveniently located near all major financial institutions and the train station. Renovations to the twenty-story luxury office building will be completed by this spring, and it will then be ready for immediate occupancy. To arrange an inspection, stop by the leasing office on the first floor today.

W: Ladies and gentlemen, before you depart, please take note of the yellow and blue sign marked *City Tour*. The bus will leave from this location at exactly 3:30 — one hour from now. Do not leave valuables on the bus. As there are many similar-looking buses, make sure you board bus number 65, with the words *Global Tours* written along the side.

M2: Aurora Textiles, the world's leading manufacturer of synthetic leather, is seeking a director of exports. The successful candidate must be willing to travel extensively and must have had experience either in the textile industry or in international marketing. Applicants should submit a resume, salary requirements, and two letters of recommendation to the personnel director by mail or fax.

ANSWERS & EXPLANATIONS

1. (D) *The meal is finished; the check and money are on the table.* Choice (A) is incorrect because the meal is over. Choice (B) is incorrect because there is no waiter in the picture. Choice (C) is incorrect because the meal has already been eaten.

2. (A) *The man has just gotten out of the car and is closing the door.* Choice (B) is incorrect because the man is not in the car. Choice (C) is incorrect because a man is getting out of the car; no one is getting in. Choice (D) is incorrect because the man is closing the door, not opening the window.

3. (C) *Several police officers are standing near their motorcycles.* Choice (A) is incorrect because the officers are talking, not directing traffic. Choice (B) is incorrect because the motorcycles are standing, not moving. Choice (D) is incorrect because the police officers are not sitting on their motorcycles.

4. (D) *The woman has her arms crossed,* meaning *folded.* Choice (A) is incorrect because there is no laundry being folded in the picture. Choice (B) is incorrect because the woman is crossing her arms, not a street. Choice (C) is incorrect because the woman is sitting, not crossing the room.

5. (C) *The baby is sitting on the woman's lap.* Choice (A) is incorrect because the baby isn't being fed. Choice (B) is incorrect because the baby is not sitting alone. Choice (D) is incorrect because the young girl is not playing with the baby.

6. (B) *The boy is riding, or sledding, down the hill on a tire.* Choice (A) is incorrect because the boy is sledding on the tire, not changing it. Choice (C) is incorrect because the tire is inflated, not flat. Choice (D) is incorrect because the boy is lying on the tire, not rolling it down the hill.

7. (D) *The flags and flagpoles are different heights.* Choice (A) is incorrect because the flags are flying on the assembled flagpoles. Choice (B) is incorrect because the flags are not flying at a lowered position. Choice (C) is incorrect because the flags are different heights.

8. (A) *The tennis match is underway; the ball is moving toward the player.* Choice (B) is incorrect because the ball is moving; it isn't in the net. Choice (C) is incorrect because the game is underway; the partners have been chosen. Choice (D) is incorrect because a racket is used in tennis, whereas a bat is used in baseball.

9. (A) *A bridge leads to the building.* Choice (B) is incorrect because the bridge is in front of the building; the building is not built on the bridge. Choice (C) is incorrect because the bridge has not been raised and no boat is passing underneath. Choice (D) is incorrect because the bridge is already built.

10. (B) *The bus has pulled up to the curb of the street.* Choice (A) is incorrect because the bus is not in motion. Choice (C) is incorrect because there are no passengers getting on the bus. Choice (D) is incorrect because the driver is not seen getting off the bus.

11. (D) *The farmers are working in the field, planting a crop.* Choice (A) is incorrect because the farmers are not working near the trees. Choice (B) is incorrect because there are no tractors in the picture. Choice (C) is incorrect because the farmers are working, not leaving the field.

12. (C) *The officer is writing a ticket that he will place on the car.* Choice (A) is incorrect because the car is not being towed. Choice (B) is incorrect because the officer is not parking the car. Choice (D) is incorrect because the officer is not writing *on* the car.

13. (B) *One man is working at a table and the other man is working at a machine.* Choice (A) is incorrect; loaves are not being packaged. Choice (C) is incorrect because only one man is working at a table. Choice (D) is incorrect because only one man is working at the machine.

14. (D) *The cars are driving side by side,* meaning *next to each other.* Choice (A) is incorrect because neither car is behind the other. Choice (B) is incorrect because the cars are moving, not parked. Choice (C) is incorrect; the cars are traveling in the same direction.

15. (B) *The men are posing for the picture by a sculpture of a duck in the park.* Choice (A) is incorrect because one man is standing. Choice (C) is incorrect because one man is sitting. Choice (D) is incorrect because the completed sculpture is of a duck, not of men.

16. (C) *The man has his feet up on the desk.* Choice (A) is incorrect because the man is reading a newspaper, not working on the computer. Choice (B) is incorrect because the man's feet are on the desk, not under it. Choice (D) is incorrect because the man is reading a newspaper, not delivering it.

17. (D) *The doctor is sitting across the table from the patient.* Choice (A) is incorrect because the patient is sitting, not getting on the table. Choice (B) is incorrect because the doctor is not checking the man's temperature. Choice (C) is incorrect because the doctor and patient are sitting, not standing.

18. (B) *The woman is telling the man something.* Choice (A) is incorrect because the woman is holding the paper, the man isn't. Choice (C) is incorrect because the woman is talking, not drawing. Choice (D) is incorrect because the woman is not on the street; they are sitting, probably in a classroom.

19. (A) *The man is ringing a bell in the street.* Choice (B) is incorrect because there is only one bell. Choice (C) is incorrect because the bell is not over the man's head. Choice (D) is incorrect because the man is ringing a bell, not a doorbell.

20. (A) *The woman is holding a brochure and showing it to the man.* Choice (B) is incorrect because the travel brochures are already hung on the wall. Choice (C) is incorrect because the woman is holding the brochure. Choice (D) is incorrect because the woman is holding a brochure, not taking ones down from a shelf.

21. (B) *I have to proofread it again* means the speaker needs to check the report one more time. Choice (A) confuses *draft* of a paper and *draft*, meaning *cold weather.* Choice (C) confuses a sport team *draft* and a sport *playoff.*

22. (B) *I try not to think about it* shows that if she were to think about the offer, she'd be sorry she hadn't taken it. Choices (A) and (C) answer a *what* question.

23. (A) *No. It must be my new hairstyle* means the man looks different because of his hair. Choice (B) answers a *do you* question. Choice (C) answers a *what kind of* question.

24. (A) *We're looking for two replacements* means they need to hire two people in the department. Choice (B) is an illogical response. Choice (C) confuses *decorator* with *design.*

25. (C) *Just about six months* means the man has been working almost six months in Singapore. Choice (A) answers a *how* question. Choice (B) answers a *when* question.

26. (C) *Every morning* means the woman checks her e-mail every day. Choice (A) answers a *do you* question. Choice (B) answers a *how long* question.

27. (B) *Actually, you can do it by phone* indicates the man can exchange his ticket over the phone and doesn't have to go the airport. Choice (A) confuses *tickets* and *train tickets.* Choice (C) answers a *how* or *what* question.

28. (C) *It's Gloria on the first floor* tells who's responsible for office supplies. Choice (A) confuses *charge* and *pay.* Choice (B) confuses *office supplies* with a related word: *copier.*

29. (A) *There's one on Second Avenue* tells where there is an open gas station. Choice (B) answers a *when* question. Choice (C) confuses *gas station* with a related activity: *change tires.*

30. (B) *Thank goodness the company did* means the man is grateful the company paid all his moving expenses. Choice (A) is illogical. Choice (C) answers a *why* question.

31. (B) *At noon on the dot* answers what time the conference call is. Choice (A) answers a *where* question. Choice (C) answers a *who* question or a *why* question.

32. (A) *Either way is fine* indicates the man has no preference for whether to drive or go by bus. Choice (B) does not answer *would you rather.* Choice (C) is an illogical response.

33. (C) *I'm not sure what the point was* means the woman was confused by the president's memo. Choices (A) and (B) answer a *when* question.

34. (A) *I'm pretty sure it is* means the woman is fairly certain that the building in question is the *Federal Reserve Bank.* Choice (B) confuses *Federal Reserve Bank* with *local bank.* Choice (C) confuses *Federal Reserve Bank* with a related word: *money.*

35. (B) *Everyone who was at the meeting* indicates those who should receive a copy of the letter. Choice (A) answers a *where* question. Choice (C) confuses *letter* with a related word: *stamp.*

36. (C) *It costs less* explains why the company decided to start manufacturing abroad. Choices (A) and (B) are illogical responses to the question.

37. (B) *No, but I'd like to try* means the woman has never played tennis on grass courts but would like to. Choice (A) confuses *tennis* with a related word: *serve.* Choice (C) confuses *grass courts* with *basketball courts.*

38. (B) *He's planning to ski in the Alps* tells where his boss is spending his winter vacation. Choice (A) is not a response to a *where* question. Choice (C) answers a *how much* question.

39. (A) *I check my guidebook* means the woman learns who to tip by looking in the guidebook. Choice (B) answers a *how much* question. Choice (C) is an illogical response.

40. (C) *We'll have to charge you for another day* means that if the woman stays in her room after checkout, she'll be charged for another night. Choice (A) answers a *what time* question. Choice (B) is an illogical response to the question.

41. (B) *At the new restaurant around the corner* tells where Joe's party is being held. Choices (A) and (C) are illogical responses to the question.

42. (A) *What a good idea* shows that the speaker agrees with the suggestion. Choices (B) and (C) answer a *when* question.

43. (B) *It's practical yet cheap* explains why the product is popular. Choice (A) answers a *when* question. Choice (C) confuses *product's popularity* with *product manager*.

44. (B) *If I'm not too busy, I can handle it* tells who will answer the phone. Choice (A) answers a *who* question. Choice (C) confuses *out sick* with a related word: *hospital*.

45. (C) *No, cash only* means one cannot pay with a credit card, only with cash. Choice (A) confuses *take credit cards*, meaning *accept them*, with *take credit for*, meaning *be responsible for*. Choice (B) confuses *credit card* with *credit department*.

46. (A) *Yes, with two sugars* means the man would like some coffee with two teaspoons of sugar. Choice (B) confuses *get some coffee*, meaning *bring the man coffee* with *get it*, meaning *understand*. Choice (C) is an illogical response to the question.

47. (B) *With a little luck* means if we're lucky we can finish by the afternoon. Choice (A) confuses *wrap up*, meaning *finish*, with *wrap the gift*. Choice (C) confuses *wrap up* with *wrapping paper is upstairs*.

48. (C) *Make sure you have all the receipts* explains that the way to submit a claim is by having the necessary receipts. Choice (A) is an illogical question in response to the question. Choice (B) answers a *do I* question.

49. (B) *It's bigger, but I want one with a window* explains why the man doesn't want to move to Jason's old office. Choice (A) answers a *where* question. Choice (C) answers a *what happened to* question.

50. (A) *Yes, it's a great place to work* answers the woman's question and then adds her opinion about the workplace. Choice (B) confuses *helpful* with *help*. Choice (C) is an illogical response to the question.

51. (C) The man is calling customer service because he doesn't know *what's wrong* with the television. Choice (A) is not mentioned. Choice (B) is incorrect because customer service answers the phone. Choice (D) confuses *snow* as the picture on the television with *snowed in*.

52. (B) The man asks *what's the next quickest way* to send the letter because he's surprised that the express cost is twenty-five dollars. Choice (A) is not mentioned. Choice (C) is contradicted by *What's the next quickest way?* Choice (D) is incorrect; he's looking for a *cheaper* way, not a *faster* way.

53. (D) The woman asks *Who does your hair?* meaning *Who is your barber/hairdresser?* Choice (A) is incorrect because she's looking for a hairdresser, not a travel agency. Choice (B) is incorrect because she's looking for a hairdresser, not South Street. Choice (C) is not mentioned.

54. (A) The woman says *I'll put an ad in this weekend's paper.* Choice (B) is incorrect because she's looking for part-time workers, not to work part-time herself. Choice (C) confuses *ship out* with a ship-related word: *cruise*. Choice (D) is contradicted by *part-time workers*.

55. (D) The man says *I meant 9:30*. Choices (A), (B), and (C) are contradicted by *I meant 9:30*.

56. (C) The man says *anything over one hundred copies has to be sent out*; therefore, one hundred is the maximum number of copies that can be made without sending the job out of the office. Choice (A) is contradicted by *anything over one hundred copies has to be sent out*. Choice (B) confuses the woman's response of *I only need to make ninety-nine* with *anything over one hundred copies has to be sent out*. Choice (D) is contradicted by *anything over one hundred copies has to be sent out*.

57. (C) The woman says *I didn't know I had to dial nine* (first). Choice (A) is incorrect because she's talking with the operator. Choice (B) is not mentioned. Choice (D) is incorrect because when the operator asks her if she dialed *nine, zero, zero, and the country code*, her response is a surprised, *oh, I didn't know I had to dial nine*, meaning she knew about the *zero, zero, and the country code*.

58. (A) When asked if he prefers any particular airline, the man responds *the fare is important to me*. When asked if he prefers any particular carrier, Choice (B), the man says *no*. The man asks the woman to check the schedule, Choice (C), but he doesn't say it's important to him. Choice (D) is not mentioned.

59. (C) The man says *I sure hope she stays longer than the last two.* Choice (A) is incorrect because the woman says Suzanne seems friendly but the man doesn't respond to the comment. Choice (B) is incorrect because the woman has already met Suzanne. Choice (D) is incorrect because he doesn't want a new operator to be found — he hopes Suzanne stays.

60. (D) When the driver is asked if there's an additional charge for sharing a cab, he responds *not if you're going to the same place.* Choices (A) and (B) are contradicted by *not if you're going to the same place.* Choice (C) is not mentioned.

61. (C) The woman will have time the next morning to go sightseeing *if they finish going over the accounts* that day; they won't be starting the budget until the next afternoon. Choice (A) is incorrect because they will *start*, not *finish* the budget the next day. Choice (B) is incorrect because they should finish the accounts that day. Choice (D) is not mentioned.

62. (D) The woman says *it's too bad they didn't go a little slower*, meaning they expanded too quickly. Choice (A) is not mentioned. Choice (B) is incorrect because she thinks the pizza place did use a market researcher. Choice (C) is not mentioned.

63. (C) *For fewer than four* (tickets), *you pay the regular price of twenty-five dollars each*, so two tickets would cost fifty dollars. Choice (A) is the price of one ticket. Choice (B) is not mentioned. Choice (D) is the price of four tickets.

64. (A) Pat Brickett is *starting her own consulting firm;* therefore, she's a consultant. Choices (B), (C), and (D) are contradicted by *she's starting her own consulting firm.*

65. (B) The man says that paying by television *is such a good idea;* he asks if she saw *how long the lines were,* indicating that it would take a long time to pay. Choice (A) is incorrect; they mention paying by Channel 3 but do not say it is tuned to the channel. Choices (C) and (D) are incorrect because additional charges *will show up on a separate bill.*

66. (D) The woman says *supposedly they use the revenue* (from the tolls) *to avoid having a state income tax.* Choices (A) and (B) are not mentioned. Although the toll booths *slow up traffic,* Choice (C), that's a result of having them, not their purpose.

67. (C) The woman says *I'm just waiting until I get my new e-mail address.* Choice (A) is not mentioned. Choice (B) is incorrect; no mention is made of an appointment with Debby. Choice (D) is incorrect; the man shows the woman his cards.

68. (A) The man asks if she's *going to check in her bag or take it on the plane.* Choice (B) is incorrect because the woman lost her suitcase once in Cairo; there's no indication that they're traveling there now. Choices (C) and (D) are contradicted by his asking if she's *going to check in her bag or take it on the plane.*

69. (B) The woman says to *make sure it's Linda* (he speaks to); *otherwise, it'll take someone new an hour just to find the paperwork.* Choices (A), (C), and (D) are contradicted by her saying to *make sure it's Linda* (he speaks to); *otherwise, it'll take someone new an hour just to find the paperwork.*

70. (C) The woman says *I try not to buy books if I can get them out of the library.* Choices (A), (B), and (D) are contradicted by her saying *I try not to buy books if I can get them out of the library.*

71. (C) The man says he *either* buys *too much* (local currency) *or not enough*, and the woman adds that *the bank charges ten percent for every transaction*, meaning they should limit the number of transactions. Choice (A) is incorrect; the woman states she doesn't know *how much local currency to buy*, but they do not go on to discuss the currency itself. Choice (B) is incorrect; they do not mention finding a different bank even though the rate is high. Choice (D) is not mentioned.

72. (A) The woman says she's *been picking up* (her paycheck) *every Friday for years*, meaning it's a habit. Choice (B) is incorrect; the man says direct deposit is simple. Choices (C) and (D) are not mentioned as reasons for her picking up the check on Fridays.

73. (B) The woman says if they *move* (from downtown), she'll *have to buy a car.* Choice (A) is incorrect because it's the man who says he loves *working downtown.* Choice (C) is incorrect because the man says he'd *hate to relocate to the suburbs.* Choice (D) is not mentioned.

74. (C) The woman says that she's the one *in charge of organizing Nancy's engagement party.* Choice (A) is incorrect because Mr. Williams has budgeted money for the party. Choice (B) is not mentioned. Choice (D) is incorrect because Mr. Williams has budgeted enough money to have the party *at the Drake Hotel.*

75. (D) The woman says *finally the office tower has some new owners.* Choices (A) and (B) are incorrect because the man says *if the place gets fixed up, the rents could be sky high.* Choice (C) is not mentioned.

76. (A) The man says *I don't know what's wrong with the one we have; it does everything I need*, meaning he sees no reason to choose another software program. Choice (B) is contradicted by *it does everything I need.* Choices (C) and (D) are not mentioned.

77. (B) When asked if the company will pay her relocation expenses, the man replies *of course.* Choice (A) is incorrect because the woman already knows *it's going to cost a fortune to move to Australia.* Choice (C) is incorrect because the woman already knows she is going *to move to Australia.* Choice (D) is incorrect because the amount of money for relocation is not fixed, *it depends on where* one is *being assigned.*

78. (C) The woman would use a pick-up service because she once *forgot to return a tape and was charged twenty-five dollars;* if the tapes were picked up, that couldn't happen. Choices (A), (B), and (D) are not mentioned.

79. (D) The man suggests that she *bring color graphics and detailed handouts,* meaning that she should have an impressive presentation. Although he tells her to *bring graphics and handouts with sales projections according to region,* he doesn't tell her to assess the projections, Choice (A), or analyze the sales, Choice (B). Choice (C) is not mentioned.

80. (B) The man asks if he'll *receive a written job description* before he begins work. Choice (A) is incorrect because he tells her he *should be done with the tour of the plant at 4:00,* at which time he'll stop by her office to get the job description. Choice (C) is not mentioned. Choice (D) is incorrect because he's beginning work; she already works there.

81. (D) *There are doors in front of the theater.* Choices (A), (B), and (C) are contradicted by the information given.

82. (B) *Please exit calmly through the doors marked* Exit. Choices (A), (C), and (D) are contradicted by *the doors marked* Exit.

83. (C) The report begins *Although these days should be the dog days of summer.* Choices (A), (B), and (D) are contradicted by *summer.*

84. (A) The report says the rain *will not end our two-month drought.* Choices (B), (C), and (D) are contradicted by *our two-month drought.*

85. (C) The announcement ends with *we will update you on the status of the thunderstorms throughout the day.* Choice (A) is incorrect; there is a chance of rain during the day but it will not be reported on. Choice (B) is incorrect; this is today's weather report — tomorrow's forecast is not mentioned. Choice (D) is incorrect; only today's temperatures have been reported.

86. (B) The speech declares that *the annual campaign has reached its goal of four million dollars.* Choice (A) is incorrect because the campaign has reached its goal; they have already raised the money. Choice (C) is incorrect because it is a *privately funded museum.* Choice (D) is not mentioned.

87. (A) The speaker says that *fund-raising campaigns are also about meeting institutional objectives.* Choice (B) is not mentioned. The *garden courtyard* will be reopened, not the museum, Choice (C). Choice (D) is not mentioned.

88. (A) *The chief goals of this campaign are to restore and reopen our garden courtyard.* Choice (B) is incorrect because the educational programs will be *improved,* not *instituted.* Choice (C) is incorrect because the collections will be *preserved,* not *added.* Choice (D) is not mentioned.

89. (B) The letter begins *Thank you for preregistering.* Choices (A) and (D) are not mentioned. Choice (C) is contradicted by *thank you for preregistering.*

90. (C) The last line is *so here's what you need to know;* presumably a list of the events follows. Choices (A) and (B) are incorrect because those receiving the letter have already preregistered. Choice (D) is incorrect because the letter informs them that *more than fifty thousand people are expected to attend.*

91. (C) *Jeffrey Stevens* had been the company's *chief executive officer since the company's inception a decade ago.* Choice (A) is incorrect because that is the year when the drug was okayed for sale in the U.S. Choice (B) is incorrect because that is the number of years Donna Cardone has been the president. Choice (D) is incorrect because that is the age at which one should take the vitamins.

92. (D) *Ever Young Pharmaceuticals announced yesterday that Jeffrey Stevens, its chief executive, had resigned.* Choices (A), (B), and (C) are contradicted by *Ever Young Pharmaceuticals announced yesterday that Jeffrey Stevens, its chief executive, had resigned.*

93. (B) Ever Young manufactures vitamins *for those over fifty.* Choices (A), (C), and (D) are contradicted by *Ever Young, one of the world's largest manufacturers of vitamins for those over fifty.*

94. (A) *M.A.S. Realty Management Corporation and Michaelson Limited Partners are pleased to announce the acquisition of 100 Church Street in Center City.* Choices (B) and (C) are not mentioned. Choice (D) is contradicted by *renovations to the twenty-story luxury office building.*

95. (C) *Renovations to the twenty-story luxury office building will be completed by this spring.* Choice (A) confuses *the leasing office on the first floor* with one floor. Choice (B) confuses *615,000 square foot office tower* with fifteen floors. Choice (D) confuses the address, *100 Church Street,* with one hundred floors.

96. (D) *Renovations will be completed by this spring, and it will then be ready for immediate occupancy.* Choice (A) is incorrect; tenants can occupy the offices immediately after the renovations are completed. Choice (B) is incorrect; potential tenants can inspect the office anytime, but renovations are not completed. Choice (C) is not mentioned.

97. (A) The announcement begins *Ladies and gentlemen, before you depart;* they are still on the bus. Choices (B) and (D) are contradicted by *ladies and gentlemen, before you depart.* Choice (C) is contradicted by *the bus will leave.*

98. (D) The people are told not to *leave valuables on the bus.* Choice (A) is incorrect because the people are told to be back *at exactly 3:30 — one hour from now.* Choice (B) is contradicted by *make sure you board bus number 65.* Choice (C) confuses *take note of,* meaning *notice,* with *take notes,* meaning *write.*

99. (A) *Aurora Textiles is seeking a director of exports.* Choices (B), (C), and (D) are contradicted by *Aurora Textiles is seeking a director of exports.*

100. (B) *Applicants should submit a resume by (mail or) fax.* Choices (A), (C), and (D) are contradicted by *applicants should submit a resume by fax.*

101. (C) The relationship between these two independent clauses is one of opposition, so *although* is the correct conjunction. Choices (A) and (D) are illogical as they introduce a clause of reason. Choice (B) is either the subject of an independent clause or, if it precedes a subject, needs to be paired with *nor.*

102. (D) *Take long,* an idiom, means *require a long time.* Choices (A), (B), and (C) are not logical.

103. (B) The comparative form of the adjective, *better,* is used with two items. Choice (A) is the superlative form. Choice (C) is the adjective form. Choice (D) is an adjective meaning *of pleasant appearance.*

104. (A) *Others* is the plural subject pronoun. Choice (B) is the singular pronoun. Choice (C) is used to refer to all of the remaining ones. Choice (D) is used before a plural or noncount noun.

105. (D) The gerund form *swimming* follows the infinitive *to spend* + a noun, *lunch hour.* Choices (A), (B), and (C) do not fit this pattern.

106. (C) *In most states* means *in the majority of states.* Choices (A) and (B) must be followed by *the.* Choice (D) is an incorrect form.

107. (B) *Ourselves* is the first-person plural reflexive pronoun which agrees with *we* and follows *by.* Choice (A) is the first-person plural object pronoun form. Choice (C) is the first-person plural possessive adjective. Choice (D) is the first-person plural subject pronoun.

108. (A) *Between* is the preposition used with two things. Choices (B) and (D) are not prepositions. Choice (C) is the preposition used with more than two things.

109. (A) *Disappointing* is used with *results* to mean that the results weren't as good as they had hoped. Choices (B), (C), and (D) are not logical.

110. (D) *The end result* is an idiom meaning *the final outcome.* Choices (A), (B), and (C) are not used with *result.*

111. (C) *About five years ago* means *five years before this time.* Choices (A), (B), and (D) are not used to convey this meaning.

112. (B) The adjective *bestselling* preceding *author* means that the author has sold a book in large numbers. Choice (A) means *disposal of commodities.* Choice (C) means *a condition with high prices and little supply.* Choice (D) means *wrapped.*

113. (C) The correct word order is verb, *ended;* adverb, *moderately;* adjective, *lower;* adverb, *today.* Choices (A), (B), and (D) are in the wrong order.

114. (D) *In the past five years* indicates the present perfect, *have risen,* is needed. Choice (A) is the past perfect passive form. Choice (B) is the gerund or active participle form. Choice (C) is the present continuous form.

115. (A) The expression *turned around* means *improved.* Choice (B) means *returned.* Choice (C) means *turned in a forward direction.* Choice (D) means *rejected.*

116. (C) A *barrier* is an *obstruction.* Choice (A) is used in geographical terms. Choices (B) and (D) are not used with *insurmountable.*

117. (C) *Evaluating the opportunity* means *assessing the circumstances.* Choice (A) refers to a person. Choice (B) means *thought.* Choice (D) is an adjective.

118. (B) In this context, only *is* is the appropriate verb. Choices (A) and (C) introduce a dependent clause. Choice (D) is the future perfect tense.

119. (A) *At the beginning* is the correct form. Choice (B) requires the preposition *in.* Choice (C) requires the preposition *on.* Choice (D) is an adjective and cannot follow the article *the* unless it is followed by a noun.

120. (D) *Single* is an adjective and can precede the noun *way.* Choice (A) is the third-person singular reflexive pronoun, which cannot precede a noun. Choice (B) is usually an adverb; when it is used as an adjective, it is not followed by a noun. Choice (C) cannnot follow *no.*

121. (C) *Than* is used with the comparison *higher.* Choices (A), (B), and (D) do not follow this pattern.

122. (B) *Bottom* is a noun, used to modify *drawer,* forming a compound noun meaning *the lowest drawer.* Choice (A) is an adverb. Choice (C) is a preposition. Choice (D) is an adverb.

123. (A) *Too little inventory* means *not enough inventory.* Choice (B) is the comparative form. Choice (C) is used with count nouns. Choice (D) is used for size, not amounts.

124. (D) *Almost everyone* means *just about every person.* Choice (A) is an adjective. Choices (B) and (C), although pronouns, are not logical.

125. (C) One *spends money on* something. Choices (A), (B), and (D) are not used with *spend.*

126. (B) *In one's old age* means *when one is old.* Although Choice (A) is a noun, it is not used to refer to age. Choice (C) is usually an adjective; when it is a noun, it is usually preceded by *the* to mean old people. Choice (D) is an adjective.

127. (A) *The time I spent* means *while I was visiting.* Choices (B), (C), and (D) are not used with *spent.*

128. (D) *Smoking is not allowed* means *smoking is not permitted.* Choice (A) is not logical. Choice (B) is used with a person. Choice (C) is not used with *smoking.*

129. (C) *That* is a relative pronoun used with things, as with *the forms.* Choices (A), (B), and (D) are not relative pronouns.

130. (B) *Looking forward to* is followed by a gerund, *concluding.* Choice (A) is the simple form. Choice (C) is a noun. Choice (D) is a prepositional phrase.

131. (D) The predicate adjective *knowledgeable* means *possessing knowledge.* Choice (A) is a noun. Choice (B) is a verb. Choice (C) is a noun.

132. (D) The adverb *so* means *in the same way.* Choice (A) is an adjective. Although Choices (B) and (C) are adverbs, they are not logical in this context.

133. (B) *In its first year of operation* means *in its first year of business.* Choice (A) means *movement from one member of a continuous series to the next.* Choice (C) means *capacity for growth.* Choice (D) means *upkeep.*

134. (B) *Venture* means *a business enterprise involving some risk in expectation of gain.* Choice (A) means *the act of making a profit.* Choice (C) means *the value of a business.* Choice (D) means *income from a particular source.*

135. (D) The adjective *occasional* describes the compound noun *sand shark.* Choice (A) is an adverb. Choice (B) is a prepositional phrase and a noun. Choice (C) is a noun.

136. (A) The reflexive pronoun *themselves* is needed. Choice (B) is a noun. Choices (C) and (D) are not logical.

137. (C) The adjective *big* modifies a noun, *problem.* Choice (A) is an adjective. Choice (B) is an adverb. Choice (D) is an adjective.

138. (B) *More studies are needed to confirm,* meaning *verify, the findings.* Choice (A) means *devise.* Choice (C) means *communicate with.* Choice (D) means *be similar to.*

139. (A) *A quarter loss* means *a three-month fall in prices.* Choices (B) and (C) are not nouns. Choice (D) is not logical.

140. (D) The active modal form of the verb, *would consolidate,* indicates a plan to consolidate. Choice (A) is the simple present. Choices (B) and (C) are passive forms.

141. (A) The adjective form is never in the plural: *two million dollars.*

142. (C) The preposition *to* is needed following *according.*

143. (C) Use the simple form of the verb after the modal *must: must complete.*

144. (D) *Repeated again* gives the same information and is redundant; use one word or the other.

145. (B) *Equipment* is a noncount noun and is always in the singular form.

146. (D) The correct preposition is *in: in the lobby.*

147. (A) Use *unlike,* the correct preposition to indicate a contrast.

148. (B) The comparative is incorrect: use *common* with *more.*

149. (D) *Enabling,* the active participle from a reduced adjective clause, is followed by a noun, *the state,* and an infinitive, *to reduce.*

150. (B) *It* is not necessary because the sentence already has a subject: *service.*

151. (B) *Mrs. Wong,* a woman, takes the feminine possessive adjective: *her.*

152. (D) An adjective is needed: *knowledgeable* should be used.

153. (A) An adjective, *no,* must precede the noun, *employee.*

154. (A) The verb *permits* is followed by a noun, *individual,* and an infinitive, *to draw up.*

155. (C) Use the person form, *architects.*

156. (B) Use the preposition *in: in two weeks.*

157. (D) *Either... or* is a paired conjunction: *either the income statement or the balance sheet.*

158. (A) Following the article, *the,* use the noun form: *majority.*

159. (C) Use the adverb form, *logically,* before the adjective, *related.*

160. (D) Use the adjective form, *other,* before the noun, *workers.*

161. (B) The title of the announcement is *When Electricom And Gasco Had The Bright Idea To Become Partners;* becoming partners is a *joint venture*. Choices (A), (C), and (D) are not mentioned.

162. (C) *Electricom wanted a partner in natural gas.* Choices (A), (B), and (D) are not mentioned.

163. (D) *Electricom can now expand its reach beyond its Michigan base*. Choice (A) is true for Gasco, not Electricom. Choice (B) is not mentioned. Choice (C) is true for Gasco, not Electricom.

164. (A) *Dan's* uses *calcium to make your teeth really clean.* Although other brands of toothpaste contain *saccharin, dyes, and preservatives* [making Choices (B), (C), and (D) incorrect], Dan's does not.

165. (C) *Try any of our other various beauty products; shampoo* is a beauty product. Choices (A), (B), and (D) are contradicted by *try any of our other various beauty products.*

166. (B) *Low prices* is not mentioned. Choices (A), (C), and (D) are explicitly mentioned.

167. (D) *Other great benefits include twenty-five percent discount at Bay Booksellers.* Choice (A) is incorrect because the discount is *ten percent*, not twenty-five percent. Choice (B) is incorrect because *coffee is free with a bakery purchase*; baked goods are not free. Choice (C) is not mentioned.

168. (A) *This is a straight donation* is one of the options. Choices (B), (C), and (D) are not mentioned.

169. (C) A Gold member pays $100. If her firm matches, Village will receive double the amount, or $200. Choices (A), (B), and (D) are contradicted by these figures.

170. (B) The brochure is called *Closet Cues: Care Labels and Your Clothes;* the brochure describes washing instructions for clothes. Choices (A), (C), and (D) are not mentioned.

171. (D) *The new symbols will no doubt cause senseless confusion as well as heartbreaking shrinkage;* clothes will not be washed as they should. Choices (A), (B) and (C) are not mentioned.

172. (C) The new brochure is *jazzy,* meaning *flashy.* Choices (A), (B), and (D) are not mentioned.

173. (A) *Throughout the summer* means the promotion will take place until the end of the summer. Choices (B), (C), and (D) are contradicted by *throughout the summer.*

174. (B) *Passengers can purchase ten minutes of domestic calls,* meaning calls anywhere in the U.S. Choices (A), (C), and (D) are not mentioned.

175. (D) *The normal charge is $2.99 per connection, plus $3.28 per minute*, meaning $12.83 for a three-minute call. Choices (A), (B), and (C) are contradicted by *the normal charge is $2.99 per connection, plus $3.28 per minute.*

176. (C) *The mark reached an eight-year high against the dollar* had happened sometime before yesterday. Choices (A), (B), and (D) are explicitly mentioned.

177. (C) *The British central bank said it had no immediate plans for future rate increases, which prompted heavy sales of pounds.* Choices (A), (B), and (D) are not mentioned.

178. (D) *The dollar fell in part on expectations that Japan's account surplus — the broadest measure of trade — had widened sharply in June.* Choices (A), (B), and (C) are contradicted by *the dollar fell in part on expectations that Japan's account surplus had widened sharply in June.*

179. (A) *A nationwide survey* was *conducted last week by a marketing research firm.* Choices (B), (C), and (D) are those who *have focused on a downward slope*, not those who conducted the survey.

180. (A) *Respondents this year who said that their standard of living is better than their parents' rose to 82 percent,* therefore, the percentage of those who said they were doing worse is 18 percent. Choices (B), (C), and (D) are contradicted by these figures.

181. (C) *Respondents in the supposedly dispirited 18- to 24-year-old age group,* means this age group is expected to be more negative. Choices (A), (B), and (D) are contradicted by *respondents in the supposedly dispirited 18- to 24-year-old age group.*

182. (D) *Respondents this year who said that their standard of living is better than their parents rose to 82 percent;* therefore, people increasingly think they are living better than their parents. Choices (A) and (B) are not mentioned. Choice (C) is contradicted by *respondents this year who said that their standard of living is better than their parents rose to 82 percent.*

183. (C) *The festival is recognized not only as one of the most important cultural events in Canada...* Choice (A) is incorrect; the films at the *World Film Festival* come from around the world. Choice (B) is incorrect because the number of countries with films represented is 63. Choice (D) confuses *throughout the western world* with *the largest film festival... in the western world.*

184. (B) Because *stars* is followed by other people: *directors, producers, writers, and fans,* these stars refer to *movie stars.* Choices (A), (C), and (D) are incorrect because of this reference.

185. (A) Because there are *670 screenings of 400 films,* some films are shown more than once. Choice (B) confuses the number of countries sending films with the number in attendance. Choice (C) is contradicted by *sixty-three countries around the world.* Choice (D) is incorrect because films will be shown, not shot, at the festival.

186. (C) The advertisement describes *the full-service business amenities you expect;* the clients are business travelers. Choices (A), (B), and (D) are contradicted by *the full-service business amenities you expect.*

187. (D) The suites are *all for the price of an ordinary hotel room.* Choices (A), (B), and (C) are contradicted by *all for the price of an ordinary hotel room.*

188. (B) The advertisement states *with nine hotels to choose from.* Choices (A) and (D) are not mentioned. Choice (C) is incorrect; the rooms can be booked by a travel agent or by calling the telephone number listed.

189. (A) *Frankfurt-based British retailer wants to establish branches in the U.S.* Choices (B), (C), and (D) are not mentioned.

190. (C) *Retailer wants to establish branches for stylish office furniture.* Choices (A), (B), and (D) are contradicted by *stylish office furniture.*

191. (D) *Ideal locations include Texas.* Choices (A), (B), and (C) are contradicted by *ideal locations include Texas.*

192. (B) The advertisement states *prefer to buy existing building.* Choices (A), (C), and (D) are contradicted by *prefer to buy existing building.*

193. (B) *In the decade of the 1980's the number of franchises abroad doubled to more than 40,000;* therefore, before that there were half as many, or *20,000.* Choice (A) is not mentioned. Choice (C) is the number of franchises in the 1980's, not before it. Choice (D) is incorrect; the number of franchises before the 1980's is half, not double, the number in the 1980's.

194. (A) *Cheaper locations* is not mentioned. Choices (B), (C), and (D) are explicitly mentioned.

195. (D) *Global franchising is, of course, a two-way street. More and more foreign franchisers are looking for franchise opportunities in the U.S.* Choices (A), (B), and (C) are contradicted by *Global franchising is, of course, a two-way street. More and more foreign franchisers are looking for franchise opportunities in the U.S.*

196. (C) *Canadian franchises enjoy the largest presence in the U.S.* Choices (A) and (D) follow Canada in the number of franchises. Choice (B) is incorrect *although successful franchises can be found on the streets of Cairo.*

197. (B) The price of *the American Eagle* increased the most; it had a $3.60 increase. Choices (A), (C), and (D) are contradicted by these figures.

198. (A) The Krugerrand's closing price is $331.50, up $3.50, making the previous price $328.00. Choices (B), (C), and (D) are contradicted by these figures.

199. (A) All of the coins are made of gold, so they are the same type of metal. Choices (B), (C), and (D) vary among the coins.

200. (D) The price per ounce of a China Panda coin today is $348.00. Choices (A), (B), and (C) are incorrect.

TEST ONE — ANSWER SHEET

Listening Comprehension

1.	Ⓐ	Ⓑ	Ⓒ	Ⓓ	35.	Ⓐ	Ⓑ	Ⓒ	Ⓓ	69.	Ⓐ	Ⓑ	Ⓒ	Ⓓ
2.	Ⓐ	Ⓑ	Ⓒ	Ⓓ	36.	Ⓐ	Ⓑ	Ⓒ	Ⓓ	70.	Ⓐ	Ⓑ	Ⓒ	Ⓓ
3.	Ⓐ	Ⓑ	Ⓒ	Ⓓ	37.	Ⓐ	Ⓑ	Ⓒ	Ⓓ	71.	Ⓐ	Ⓑ	Ⓒ	Ⓓ
4.	Ⓐ	Ⓑ	Ⓒ	Ⓓ	38.	Ⓐ	Ⓑ	Ⓒ	Ⓓ	72.	Ⓐ	Ⓑ	Ⓒ	Ⓓ
5.	Ⓐ	Ⓑ	Ⓒ	Ⓓ	39.	Ⓐ	Ⓑ	Ⓒ	Ⓓ	73.	Ⓐ	Ⓑ	Ⓒ	Ⓓ
6.	Ⓐ	Ⓑ	Ⓒ	Ⓓ	40.	Ⓐ	Ⓑ	Ⓒ	Ⓓ	74.	Ⓐ	Ⓑ	Ⓒ	Ⓓ
7.	Ⓐ	Ⓑ	Ⓒ	Ⓓ	41.	Ⓐ	Ⓑ	Ⓒ	Ⓓ	75.	Ⓐ	Ⓑ	Ⓒ	Ⓓ
8.	Ⓐ	Ⓑ	Ⓒ	Ⓓ	42.	Ⓐ	Ⓑ	Ⓒ	Ⓓ	76.	Ⓐ	Ⓑ	Ⓒ	Ⓓ
9.	Ⓐ	Ⓑ	Ⓒ	Ⓓ	43.	Ⓐ	Ⓑ	Ⓒ	Ⓓ	77.	Ⓐ	Ⓑ	Ⓒ	Ⓓ
10.	Ⓐ	Ⓑ	Ⓒ	Ⓓ	44.	Ⓐ	Ⓑ	Ⓒ	Ⓓ	78.	Ⓐ	Ⓑ	Ⓒ	Ⓓ
11.	Ⓐ	Ⓑ	Ⓒ	Ⓓ	45.	Ⓐ	Ⓑ	Ⓒ	Ⓓ	79.	Ⓐ	Ⓑ	Ⓒ	Ⓓ
12.	Ⓐ	Ⓑ	Ⓒ	Ⓓ	46.	Ⓐ	Ⓑ	Ⓒ	Ⓓ	80.	Ⓐ	Ⓑ	Ⓒ	Ⓓ
13.	Ⓐ	Ⓑ	Ⓒ	Ⓓ	47.	Ⓐ	Ⓑ	Ⓒ	Ⓓ	81.	Ⓐ	Ⓑ	Ⓒ	Ⓓ
14.	Ⓐ	Ⓑ	Ⓒ	Ⓓ	48.	Ⓐ	Ⓑ	Ⓒ	Ⓓ	82.	Ⓐ	Ⓑ	Ⓒ	Ⓓ
15.	Ⓐ	Ⓑ	Ⓒ	Ⓓ	49.	Ⓐ	Ⓑ	Ⓒ	Ⓓ	83.	Ⓐ	Ⓑ	Ⓒ	Ⓓ
16.	Ⓐ	Ⓑ	Ⓒ	Ⓓ	50.	Ⓐ	Ⓑ	Ⓒ	Ⓓ	84.	Ⓐ	Ⓑ	Ⓒ	Ⓓ
17.	Ⓐ	Ⓑ	Ⓒ	Ⓓ	51.	Ⓐ	Ⓑ	Ⓒ	Ⓓ	85.	Ⓐ	Ⓑ	Ⓒ	Ⓓ
18.	Ⓐ	Ⓑ	Ⓒ	Ⓓ	52.	Ⓐ	Ⓑ	Ⓒ	Ⓓ	86.	Ⓐ	Ⓑ	Ⓒ	Ⓓ
19.	Ⓐ	Ⓑ	Ⓒ	Ⓓ	53.	Ⓐ	Ⓑ	Ⓒ	Ⓓ	87.	Ⓐ	Ⓑ	Ⓒ	Ⓓ
20.	Ⓐ	Ⓑ	Ⓒ	Ⓓ	54.	Ⓐ	Ⓑ	Ⓒ	Ⓓ	88.	Ⓐ	Ⓑ	Ⓒ	Ⓓ
21.	Ⓐ	Ⓑ	Ⓒ	Ⓓ	55.	Ⓐ	Ⓑ	Ⓒ	Ⓓ	89.	Ⓐ	Ⓑ	Ⓒ	Ⓓ
22.	Ⓐ	Ⓑ	Ⓒ	Ⓓ	56.	Ⓐ	Ⓑ	Ⓒ	Ⓓ	90.	Ⓐ	Ⓑ	Ⓒ	Ⓓ
23.	Ⓐ	Ⓑ	Ⓒ	Ⓓ	57.	Ⓐ	Ⓑ	Ⓒ	Ⓓ	91.	Ⓐ	Ⓑ	Ⓒ	Ⓓ
24.	Ⓐ	Ⓑ	Ⓒ	Ⓓ	58.	Ⓐ	Ⓑ	Ⓒ	Ⓓ	92.	Ⓐ	Ⓑ	Ⓒ	Ⓓ
25.	Ⓐ	Ⓑ	Ⓒ	Ⓓ	59.	Ⓐ	Ⓑ	Ⓒ	Ⓓ	93.	Ⓐ	Ⓑ	Ⓒ	Ⓓ
26.	Ⓐ	Ⓑ	Ⓒ	Ⓓ	60.	Ⓐ	Ⓑ	Ⓒ	Ⓓ	94.	Ⓐ	Ⓑ	Ⓒ	Ⓓ
27.	Ⓐ	Ⓑ	Ⓒ	Ⓓ	61.	Ⓐ	Ⓑ	Ⓒ	Ⓓ	95.	Ⓐ	Ⓑ	Ⓒ	Ⓓ
28.	Ⓐ	Ⓑ	Ⓒ	Ⓓ	62.	Ⓐ	Ⓑ	Ⓒ	Ⓓ	96.	Ⓐ	Ⓑ	Ⓒ	Ⓓ
29.	Ⓐ	Ⓑ	Ⓒ	Ⓓ	63.	Ⓐ	Ⓑ	Ⓒ	Ⓓ	97.	Ⓐ	Ⓑ	Ⓒ	Ⓓ
30.	Ⓐ	Ⓑ	Ⓒ	Ⓓ	64.	Ⓐ	Ⓑ	Ⓒ	Ⓓ	98.	Ⓐ	Ⓑ	Ⓒ	Ⓓ
31.	Ⓐ	Ⓑ	Ⓒ	Ⓓ	65.	Ⓐ	Ⓑ	Ⓒ	Ⓓ	99.	Ⓐ	Ⓑ	Ⓒ	Ⓓ
32.	Ⓐ	Ⓑ	Ⓒ	Ⓓ	66.	Ⓐ	Ⓑ	Ⓒ	Ⓓ	100.	Ⓐ	Ⓑ	Ⓒ	Ⓓ
33.	Ⓐ	Ⓑ	Ⓒ	Ⓓ	67.	Ⓐ	Ⓑ	Ⓒ	Ⓓ					
34.	Ⓐ	Ⓑ	Ⓒ	Ⓓ	68.	Ⓐ	Ⓑ	Ⓒ	Ⓓ					

Reading Comprehension

101. Ⓐ Ⓑ Ⓒ Ⓓ	135. Ⓐ Ⓑ Ⓒ Ⓓ	169. Ⓐ Ⓑ Ⓒ Ⓓ
102. Ⓐ Ⓑ Ⓒ Ⓓ	136. Ⓐ Ⓑ Ⓒ Ⓓ	170. Ⓐ Ⓑ Ⓒ Ⓓ
103. Ⓐ Ⓑ Ⓒ Ⓓ	137. Ⓐ Ⓑ Ⓒ Ⓓ	171. Ⓐ Ⓑ Ⓒ Ⓓ
104. Ⓐ Ⓑ Ⓒ Ⓓ	138. Ⓐ Ⓑ Ⓒ Ⓓ	172. Ⓐ Ⓑ Ⓒ Ⓓ
105. Ⓐ Ⓑ Ⓒ Ⓓ	139. Ⓐ Ⓑ Ⓒ Ⓓ	173. Ⓐ Ⓑ Ⓒ Ⓓ
106. Ⓐ Ⓑ Ⓒ Ⓓ	140. Ⓐ Ⓑ Ⓒ Ⓓ	174. Ⓐ Ⓑ Ⓒ Ⓓ
107. Ⓐ Ⓑ Ⓒ Ⓓ	141. Ⓐ Ⓑ Ⓒ Ⓓ	175. Ⓐ Ⓑ Ⓒ Ⓓ
108. Ⓐ Ⓑ Ⓒ Ⓓ	142. Ⓐ Ⓑ Ⓒ Ⓓ	176. Ⓐ Ⓑ Ⓒ Ⓓ
109. Ⓐ Ⓑ Ⓒ Ⓓ	143. Ⓐ Ⓑ Ⓒ Ⓓ	177. Ⓐ Ⓑ Ⓒ Ⓓ
110. Ⓐ Ⓑ Ⓒ Ⓓ	144. Ⓐ Ⓑ Ⓒ Ⓓ	178. Ⓐ Ⓑ Ⓒ Ⓓ
111. Ⓐ Ⓑ Ⓒ Ⓓ	145. Ⓐ Ⓑ Ⓒ Ⓓ	179. Ⓐ Ⓑ Ⓒ Ⓓ
112. Ⓐ Ⓑ Ⓒ Ⓓ	146. Ⓐ Ⓑ Ⓒ Ⓓ	180. Ⓐ Ⓑ Ⓒ Ⓓ
113. Ⓐ Ⓑ Ⓒ Ⓓ	147. Ⓐ Ⓑ Ⓒ Ⓓ	181. Ⓐ Ⓑ Ⓒ Ⓓ
114. Ⓐ Ⓑ Ⓒ Ⓓ	148. Ⓐ Ⓑ Ⓒ Ⓓ	182. Ⓐ Ⓑ Ⓒ Ⓓ
115. Ⓐ Ⓑ Ⓒ Ⓓ	149. Ⓐ Ⓑ Ⓒ Ⓓ	183. Ⓐ Ⓑ Ⓒ Ⓓ
116. Ⓐ Ⓑ Ⓒ Ⓓ	150. Ⓐ Ⓑ Ⓒ Ⓓ	184. Ⓐ Ⓑ Ⓒ Ⓓ
117. Ⓐ Ⓑ Ⓒ Ⓓ	151. Ⓐ Ⓑ Ⓒ Ⓓ	185. Ⓐ Ⓑ Ⓒ Ⓓ
118. Ⓐ Ⓑ Ⓒ Ⓓ	152. Ⓐ Ⓑ Ⓒ Ⓓ	186. Ⓐ Ⓑ Ⓒ Ⓓ
119. Ⓐ Ⓑ Ⓒ Ⓓ	153. Ⓐ Ⓑ Ⓒ Ⓓ	187. Ⓐ Ⓑ Ⓒ Ⓓ
120. Ⓐ Ⓑ Ⓒ Ⓓ	154. Ⓐ Ⓑ Ⓒ Ⓓ	188. Ⓐ Ⓑ Ⓒ Ⓓ
121. Ⓐ Ⓑ Ⓒ Ⓓ	155. Ⓐ Ⓑ Ⓒ Ⓓ	189. Ⓐ Ⓑ Ⓒ Ⓓ
122. Ⓐ Ⓑ Ⓒ Ⓓ	156. Ⓐ Ⓑ Ⓒ Ⓓ	190. Ⓐ Ⓑ Ⓒ Ⓓ
123. Ⓐ Ⓑ Ⓒ Ⓓ	157. Ⓐ Ⓑ Ⓒ Ⓓ	191. Ⓐ Ⓑ Ⓒ Ⓓ
124. Ⓐ Ⓑ Ⓒ Ⓓ	158. Ⓐ Ⓑ Ⓒ Ⓓ	192. Ⓐ Ⓑ Ⓒ Ⓓ
125. Ⓐ Ⓑ Ⓒ Ⓓ	159. Ⓐ Ⓑ Ⓒ Ⓓ	193. Ⓐ Ⓑ Ⓒ Ⓓ
126. Ⓐ Ⓑ Ⓒ Ⓓ	160. Ⓐ Ⓑ Ⓒ Ⓓ	194. Ⓐ Ⓑ Ⓒ Ⓓ
127. Ⓐ Ⓑ Ⓒ Ⓓ	161. Ⓐ Ⓑ Ⓒ Ⓓ	195. Ⓐ Ⓑ Ⓒ Ⓓ
128. Ⓐ Ⓑ Ⓒ Ⓓ	162. Ⓐ Ⓑ Ⓒ Ⓓ	196. Ⓐ Ⓑ Ⓒ Ⓓ
129. Ⓐ Ⓑ Ⓒ Ⓓ	163. Ⓐ Ⓑ Ⓒ Ⓓ	197. Ⓐ Ⓑ Ⓒ Ⓓ
130. Ⓐ Ⓑ Ⓒ Ⓓ	164. Ⓐ Ⓑ Ⓒ Ⓓ	198. Ⓐ Ⓑ Ⓒ Ⓓ
131. Ⓐ Ⓑ Ⓒ Ⓓ	165. Ⓐ Ⓑ Ⓒ Ⓓ	199. Ⓐ Ⓑ Ⓒ Ⓓ
132. Ⓐ Ⓑ Ⓒ Ⓓ	166. Ⓐ Ⓑ Ⓒ Ⓓ	200. Ⓐ Ⓑ Ⓒ Ⓓ
133. Ⓐ Ⓑ Ⓒ Ⓓ	167. Ⓐ Ⓑ Ⓒ Ⓓ	
134. Ⓐ Ⓑ Ⓒ Ⓓ	168. Ⓐ Ⓑ Ⓒ Ⓓ	

TEST TWO — ANSWER SHEET

Listening Comprehension

1.	Ⓐ	Ⓑ	Ⓒ	Ⓓ	35.	Ⓐ	Ⓑ	Ⓒ	Ⓓ	69.	Ⓐ	Ⓑ	Ⓒ	Ⓓ
2.	Ⓐ	Ⓑ	Ⓒ	Ⓓ	36.	Ⓐ	Ⓑ	Ⓒ	Ⓓ	70.	Ⓐ	Ⓑ	Ⓒ	Ⓓ
3.	Ⓐ	Ⓑ	Ⓒ	Ⓓ	37.	Ⓐ	Ⓑ	Ⓒ	Ⓓ	71.	Ⓐ	Ⓑ	Ⓒ	Ⓓ
4.	Ⓐ	Ⓑ	Ⓒ	Ⓓ	38.	Ⓐ	Ⓑ	Ⓒ	Ⓓ	72.	Ⓐ	Ⓑ	Ⓒ	Ⓓ
5.	Ⓐ	Ⓑ	Ⓒ	Ⓓ	39.	Ⓐ	Ⓑ	Ⓒ	Ⓓ	73.	Ⓐ	Ⓑ	Ⓒ	Ⓓ
6.	Ⓐ	Ⓑ	Ⓒ	Ⓓ	40.	Ⓐ	Ⓑ	Ⓒ	Ⓓ	74.	Ⓐ	Ⓑ	Ⓒ	Ⓓ
7.	Ⓐ	Ⓑ	Ⓒ	Ⓓ	41.	Ⓐ	Ⓑ	Ⓒ	Ⓓ	75.	Ⓐ	Ⓑ	Ⓒ	Ⓓ
8.	Ⓐ	Ⓑ	Ⓒ	Ⓓ	42.	Ⓐ	Ⓑ	Ⓒ	Ⓓ	76.	Ⓐ	Ⓑ	Ⓒ	Ⓓ
9.	Ⓐ	Ⓑ	Ⓒ	Ⓓ	43.	Ⓐ	Ⓑ	Ⓒ	Ⓓ	77.	Ⓐ	Ⓑ	Ⓒ	Ⓓ
10.	Ⓐ	Ⓑ	Ⓒ	Ⓓ	44.	Ⓐ	Ⓑ	Ⓒ	Ⓓ	78.	Ⓐ	Ⓑ	Ⓒ	Ⓓ
11.	Ⓐ	Ⓑ	Ⓒ	Ⓓ	45.	Ⓐ	Ⓑ	Ⓒ	Ⓓ	79.	Ⓐ	Ⓑ	Ⓒ	Ⓓ
12.	Ⓐ	Ⓑ	Ⓒ	Ⓓ	46.	Ⓐ	Ⓑ	Ⓒ	Ⓓ	80.	Ⓐ	Ⓑ	Ⓒ	Ⓓ
13.	Ⓐ	Ⓑ	Ⓒ	Ⓓ	47.	Ⓐ	Ⓑ	Ⓒ	Ⓓ	81.	Ⓐ	Ⓑ	Ⓒ	Ⓓ
14.	Ⓐ	Ⓑ	Ⓒ	Ⓓ	48.	Ⓐ	Ⓑ	Ⓒ	Ⓓ	82.	Ⓐ	Ⓑ	Ⓒ	Ⓓ
15.	Ⓐ	Ⓑ	Ⓒ	Ⓓ	49.	Ⓐ	Ⓑ	Ⓒ	Ⓓ	83.	Ⓐ	Ⓑ	Ⓒ	Ⓓ
16.	Ⓐ	Ⓑ	Ⓒ	Ⓓ	50.	Ⓐ	Ⓑ	Ⓒ	Ⓓ	84.	Ⓐ	Ⓑ	Ⓒ	Ⓓ
17.	Ⓐ	Ⓑ	Ⓒ	Ⓓ	51.	Ⓐ	Ⓑ	Ⓒ	Ⓓ	85.	Ⓐ	Ⓑ	Ⓒ	Ⓓ
18.	Ⓐ	Ⓑ	Ⓒ	Ⓓ	52.	Ⓐ	Ⓑ	Ⓒ	Ⓓ	86.	Ⓐ	Ⓑ	Ⓒ	Ⓓ
19.	Ⓐ	Ⓑ	Ⓒ	Ⓓ	53.	Ⓐ	Ⓑ	Ⓒ	Ⓓ	87.	Ⓐ	Ⓑ	Ⓒ	Ⓓ
20.	Ⓐ	Ⓑ	Ⓒ	Ⓓ	54.	Ⓐ	Ⓑ	Ⓒ	Ⓓ	88.	Ⓐ	Ⓑ	Ⓒ	Ⓓ
21.	Ⓐ	Ⓑ	Ⓒ	Ⓓ	55.	Ⓐ	Ⓑ	Ⓒ	Ⓓ	89.	Ⓐ	Ⓑ	Ⓒ	Ⓓ
22.	Ⓐ	Ⓑ	Ⓒ	Ⓓ	56.	Ⓐ	Ⓑ	Ⓒ	Ⓓ	90.	Ⓐ	Ⓑ	Ⓒ	Ⓓ
23.	Ⓐ	Ⓑ	Ⓒ	Ⓓ	57.	Ⓐ	Ⓑ	Ⓒ	Ⓓ	91.	Ⓐ	Ⓑ	Ⓒ	Ⓓ
24.	Ⓐ	Ⓑ	Ⓒ	Ⓓ	58.	Ⓐ	Ⓑ	Ⓒ	Ⓓ	92.	Ⓐ	Ⓑ	Ⓒ	Ⓓ
25.	Ⓐ	Ⓑ	Ⓒ	Ⓓ	59.	Ⓐ	Ⓑ	Ⓒ	Ⓓ	93.	Ⓐ	Ⓑ	Ⓒ	Ⓓ
26.	Ⓐ	Ⓑ	Ⓒ	Ⓓ	60.	Ⓐ	Ⓑ	Ⓒ	Ⓓ	94.	Ⓐ	Ⓑ	Ⓒ	Ⓓ
27.	Ⓐ	Ⓑ	Ⓒ	Ⓓ	61.	Ⓐ	Ⓑ	Ⓒ	Ⓓ	95.	Ⓐ	Ⓑ	Ⓒ	Ⓓ
28.	Ⓐ	Ⓑ	Ⓒ	Ⓓ	62.	Ⓐ	Ⓑ	Ⓒ	Ⓓ	96.	Ⓐ	Ⓑ	Ⓒ	Ⓓ
29.	Ⓐ	Ⓑ	Ⓒ	Ⓓ	63.	Ⓐ	Ⓑ	Ⓒ	Ⓓ	97.	Ⓐ	Ⓑ	Ⓒ	Ⓓ
30.	Ⓐ	Ⓑ	Ⓒ	Ⓓ	64.	Ⓐ	Ⓑ	Ⓒ	Ⓓ	98.	Ⓐ	Ⓑ	Ⓒ	Ⓓ
31.	Ⓐ	Ⓑ	Ⓒ	Ⓓ	65.	Ⓐ	Ⓑ	Ⓒ	Ⓓ	99.	Ⓐ	Ⓑ	Ⓒ	Ⓓ
32.	Ⓐ	Ⓑ	Ⓒ	Ⓓ	66.	Ⓐ	Ⓑ	Ⓒ	Ⓓ	100.	Ⓐ	Ⓑ	Ⓒ	Ⓓ
33.	Ⓐ	Ⓑ	Ⓒ	Ⓓ	67.	Ⓐ	Ⓑ	Ⓒ	Ⓓ					
34.	Ⓐ	Ⓑ	Ⓒ	Ⓓ	68.	Ⓐ	Ⓑ	Ⓒ	Ⓓ					

Reading Comprehension

101. Ⓐ Ⓑ Ⓒ Ⓓ	135. Ⓐ Ⓑ Ⓒ Ⓓ	169. Ⓐ Ⓑ Ⓒ Ⓓ
102. Ⓐ Ⓑ Ⓒ Ⓓ	136. Ⓐ Ⓑ Ⓒ Ⓓ	170. Ⓐ Ⓑ Ⓒ Ⓓ
103. Ⓐ Ⓑ Ⓒ Ⓓ	137. Ⓐ Ⓑ Ⓒ Ⓓ	171. Ⓐ Ⓑ Ⓒ Ⓓ
104. Ⓐ Ⓑ Ⓒ Ⓓ	138. Ⓐ Ⓑ Ⓒ Ⓓ	172. Ⓐ Ⓑ Ⓒ Ⓓ
105. Ⓐ Ⓑ Ⓒ Ⓓ	139. Ⓐ Ⓑ Ⓒ Ⓓ	173. Ⓐ Ⓑ Ⓒ Ⓓ
106. Ⓐ Ⓑ Ⓒ Ⓓ	140. Ⓐ Ⓑ Ⓒ Ⓓ	174. Ⓐ Ⓑ Ⓒ Ⓓ
107. Ⓐ Ⓑ Ⓒ Ⓓ	141. Ⓐ Ⓑ Ⓒ Ⓓ	175. Ⓐ Ⓑ Ⓒ Ⓓ
108. Ⓐ Ⓑ Ⓒ Ⓓ	142. Ⓐ Ⓑ Ⓒ Ⓓ	176. Ⓐ Ⓑ Ⓒ Ⓓ
109. Ⓐ Ⓑ Ⓒ Ⓓ	143. Ⓐ Ⓑ Ⓒ Ⓓ	177. Ⓐ Ⓑ Ⓒ Ⓓ
110. Ⓐ Ⓑ Ⓒ Ⓓ	144. Ⓐ Ⓑ Ⓒ Ⓓ	178. Ⓐ Ⓑ Ⓒ Ⓓ
111. Ⓐ Ⓑ Ⓒ Ⓓ	145. Ⓐ Ⓑ Ⓒ Ⓓ	179. Ⓐ Ⓑ Ⓒ Ⓓ
112. Ⓐ Ⓑ Ⓒ Ⓓ	146. Ⓐ Ⓑ Ⓒ Ⓓ	180. Ⓐ Ⓑ Ⓒ Ⓓ
113. Ⓐ Ⓑ Ⓒ Ⓓ	147. Ⓐ Ⓑ Ⓒ Ⓓ	181. Ⓐ Ⓑ Ⓒ Ⓓ
114. Ⓐ Ⓑ Ⓒ Ⓓ	148. Ⓐ Ⓑ Ⓒ Ⓓ	182. Ⓐ Ⓑ Ⓒ Ⓓ
115. Ⓐ Ⓑ Ⓒ Ⓓ	149. Ⓐ Ⓑ Ⓒ Ⓓ	183. Ⓐ Ⓑ Ⓒ Ⓓ
116. Ⓐ Ⓑ Ⓒ Ⓓ	150. Ⓐ Ⓑ Ⓒ Ⓓ	184. Ⓐ Ⓑ Ⓒ Ⓓ
117. Ⓐ Ⓑ Ⓒ Ⓓ	151. Ⓐ Ⓑ Ⓒ Ⓓ	185. Ⓐ Ⓑ Ⓒ Ⓓ
118. Ⓐ Ⓑ Ⓒ Ⓓ	152. Ⓐ Ⓑ Ⓒ Ⓓ	186. Ⓐ Ⓑ Ⓒ Ⓓ
119. Ⓐ Ⓑ Ⓒ Ⓓ	153. Ⓐ Ⓑ Ⓒ Ⓓ	187. Ⓐ Ⓑ Ⓒ Ⓓ
120. Ⓐ Ⓑ Ⓒ Ⓓ	154. Ⓐ Ⓑ Ⓒ Ⓓ	188. Ⓐ Ⓑ Ⓒ Ⓓ
121. Ⓐ Ⓑ Ⓒ Ⓓ	155. Ⓐ Ⓑ Ⓒ Ⓓ	189. Ⓐ Ⓑ Ⓒ Ⓓ
122. Ⓐ Ⓑ Ⓒ Ⓓ	156. Ⓐ Ⓑ Ⓒ Ⓓ	190. Ⓐ Ⓑ Ⓒ Ⓓ
123. Ⓐ Ⓑ Ⓒ Ⓓ	157. Ⓐ Ⓑ Ⓒ Ⓓ	191. Ⓐ Ⓑ Ⓒ Ⓓ
124. Ⓐ Ⓑ Ⓒ Ⓓ	158. Ⓐ Ⓑ Ⓒ Ⓓ	192. Ⓐ Ⓑ Ⓒ Ⓓ
125. Ⓐ Ⓑ Ⓒ Ⓓ	159. Ⓐ Ⓑ Ⓒ Ⓓ	193. Ⓐ Ⓑ Ⓒ Ⓓ
126. Ⓐ Ⓑ Ⓒ Ⓓ	160. Ⓐ Ⓑ Ⓒ Ⓓ	194. Ⓐ Ⓑ Ⓒ Ⓓ
127. Ⓐ Ⓑ Ⓒ Ⓓ	161. Ⓐ Ⓑ Ⓒ Ⓓ	195. Ⓐ Ⓑ Ⓒ Ⓓ
128. Ⓐ Ⓑ Ⓒ Ⓓ	162. Ⓐ Ⓑ Ⓒ Ⓓ	196. Ⓐ Ⓑ Ⓒ Ⓓ
129. Ⓐ Ⓑ Ⓒ Ⓓ	163. Ⓐ Ⓑ Ⓒ Ⓓ	197. Ⓐ Ⓑ Ⓒ Ⓓ
130. Ⓐ Ⓑ Ⓒ Ⓓ	164. Ⓐ Ⓑ Ⓒ Ⓓ	198. Ⓐ Ⓑ Ⓒ Ⓓ
131. Ⓐ Ⓑ Ⓒ Ⓓ	165. Ⓐ Ⓑ Ⓒ Ⓓ	199. Ⓐ Ⓑ Ⓒ Ⓓ
132. Ⓐ Ⓑ Ⓒ Ⓓ	166. Ⓐ Ⓑ Ⓒ Ⓓ	200. Ⓐ Ⓑ Ⓒ Ⓓ
133. Ⓐ Ⓑ Ⓒ Ⓓ	167. Ⓐ Ⓑ Ⓒ Ⓓ	
134. Ⓐ Ⓑ Ⓒ Ⓓ	168. Ⓐ Ⓑ Ⓒ Ⓓ	

TEST THREE — ANSWER SHEET

Listening Comprehension

1.	Ⓐ	Ⓑ	Ⓒ	Ⓓ	35.	Ⓐ	Ⓑ	Ⓒ	Ⓓ	69.	Ⓐ	Ⓑ	Ⓒ	Ⓓ
2.	Ⓐ	Ⓑ	Ⓒ	Ⓓ	36.	Ⓐ	Ⓑ	Ⓒ	Ⓓ	70.	Ⓐ	Ⓑ	Ⓒ	Ⓓ
3.	Ⓐ	Ⓑ	Ⓒ	Ⓓ	37.	Ⓐ	Ⓑ	Ⓒ	Ⓓ	71.	Ⓐ	Ⓑ	Ⓒ	Ⓓ
4.	Ⓐ	Ⓑ	Ⓒ	Ⓓ	38.	Ⓐ	Ⓑ	Ⓒ	Ⓓ	72.	Ⓐ	Ⓑ	Ⓒ	Ⓓ
5.	Ⓐ	Ⓑ	Ⓒ	Ⓓ	39.	Ⓐ	Ⓑ	Ⓒ	Ⓓ	73.	Ⓐ	Ⓑ	Ⓒ	Ⓓ
6.	Ⓐ	Ⓑ	Ⓒ	Ⓓ	40.	Ⓐ	Ⓑ	Ⓒ	Ⓓ	74.	Ⓐ	Ⓑ	Ⓒ	Ⓓ
7.	Ⓐ	Ⓑ	Ⓒ	Ⓓ	41.	Ⓐ	Ⓑ	Ⓒ	Ⓓ	75.	Ⓐ	Ⓑ	Ⓒ	Ⓓ
8.	Ⓐ	Ⓑ	Ⓒ	Ⓓ	42.	Ⓐ	Ⓑ	Ⓒ	Ⓓ	76.	Ⓐ	Ⓑ	Ⓒ	Ⓓ
9.	Ⓐ	Ⓑ	Ⓒ	Ⓓ	43.	Ⓐ	Ⓑ	Ⓒ	Ⓓ	77.	Ⓐ	Ⓑ	Ⓒ	Ⓓ
10.	Ⓐ	Ⓑ	Ⓒ	Ⓓ	44.	Ⓐ	Ⓑ	Ⓒ	Ⓓ	78.	Ⓐ	Ⓑ	Ⓒ	Ⓓ
11.	Ⓐ	Ⓑ	Ⓒ	Ⓓ	45.	Ⓐ	Ⓑ	Ⓒ	Ⓓ	79.	Ⓐ	Ⓑ	Ⓒ	Ⓓ
12.	Ⓐ	Ⓑ	Ⓒ	Ⓓ	46.	Ⓐ	Ⓑ	Ⓒ	Ⓓ	80.	Ⓐ	Ⓑ	Ⓒ	Ⓓ
13.	Ⓐ	Ⓑ	Ⓒ	Ⓓ	47.	Ⓐ	Ⓑ	Ⓒ	Ⓓ	81.	Ⓐ	Ⓑ	Ⓒ	Ⓓ
14.	Ⓐ	Ⓑ	Ⓒ	Ⓓ	48.	Ⓐ	Ⓑ	Ⓒ	Ⓓ	82.	Ⓐ	Ⓑ	Ⓒ	Ⓓ
15.	Ⓐ	Ⓑ	Ⓒ	Ⓓ	49.	Ⓐ	Ⓑ	Ⓒ	Ⓓ	83.	Ⓐ	Ⓑ	Ⓒ	Ⓓ
16.	Ⓐ	Ⓑ	Ⓒ	Ⓓ	50.	Ⓐ	Ⓑ	Ⓒ	Ⓓ	84.	Ⓐ	Ⓑ	Ⓒ	Ⓓ
17.	Ⓐ	Ⓑ	Ⓒ	Ⓓ	51.	Ⓐ	Ⓑ	Ⓒ	Ⓓ	85.	Ⓐ	Ⓑ	Ⓒ	Ⓓ
18.	Ⓐ	Ⓑ	Ⓒ	Ⓓ	52.	Ⓐ	Ⓑ	Ⓒ	Ⓓ	86.	Ⓐ	Ⓑ	Ⓒ	Ⓓ
19.	Ⓐ	Ⓑ	Ⓒ	Ⓓ	53.	Ⓐ	Ⓑ	Ⓒ	Ⓓ	87.	Ⓐ	Ⓑ	Ⓒ	Ⓓ
20.	Ⓐ	Ⓑ	Ⓒ	Ⓓ	54.	Ⓐ	Ⓑ	Ⓒ	Ⓓ	88.	Ⓐ	Ⓑ	Ⓒ	Ⓓ
21.	Ⓐ	Ⓑ	Ⓒ	Ⓓ	55.	Ⓐ	Ⓑ	Ⓒ	Ⓓ	89.	Ⓐ	Ⓑ	Ⓒ	Ⓓ
22.	Ⓐ	Ⓑ	Ⓒ	Ⓓ	56.	Ⓐ	Ⓑ	Ⓒ	Ⓓ	90.	Ⓐ	Ⓑ	Ⓒ	Ⓓ
23.	Ⓐ	Ⓑ	Ⓒ	Ⓓ	57.	Ⓐ	Ⓑ	Ⓒ	Ⓓ	91.	Ⓐ	Ⓑ	Ⓒ	Ⓓ
24.	Ⓐ	Ⓑ	Ⓒ	Ⓓ	58.	Ⓐ	Ⓑ	Ⓒ	Ⓓ	92.	Ⓐ	Ⓑ	Ⓒ	Ⓓ
25.	Ⓐ	Ⓑ	Ⓒ	Ⓓ	59.	Ⓐ	Ⓑ	Ⓒ	Ⓓ	93.	Ⓐ	Ⓑ	Ⓒ	Ⓓ
26.	Ⓐ	Ⓑ	Ⓒ	Ⓓ	60.	Ⓐ	Ⓑ	Ⓒ	Ⓓ	94.	Ⓐ	Ⓑ	Ⓒ	Ⓓ
27.	Ⓐ	Ⓑ	Ⓒ	Ⓓ	61.	Ⓐ	Ⓑ	Ⓒ	Ⓓ	95.	Ⓐ	Ⓑ	Ⓒ	Ⓓ
28.	Ⓐ	Ⓑ	Ⓒ	Ⓓ	62.	Ⓐ	Ⓑ	Ⓒ	Ⓓ	96.	Ⓐ	Ⓑ	Ⓒ	Ⓓ
29.	Ⓐ	Ⓑ	Ⓒ	Ⓓ	63.	Ⓐ	Ⓑ	Ⓒ	Ⓓ	97.	Ⓐ	Ⓑ	Ⓒ	Ⓓ
30.	Ⓐ	Ⓑ	Ⓒ	Ⓓ	64.	Ⓐ	Ⓑ	Ⓒ	Ⓓ	98.	Ⓐ	Ⓑ	Ⓒ	Ⓓ
31.	Ⓐ	Ⓑ	Ⓒ	Ⓓ	65.	Ⓐ	Ⓑ	Ⓒ	Ⓓ	99.	Ⓐ	Ⓑ	Ⓒ	Ⓓ
32.	Ⓐ	Ⓑ	Ⓒ	Ⓓ	66.	Ⓐ	Ⓑ	Ⓒ	Ⓓ	100.	Ⓐ	Ⓑ	Ⓒ	Ⓓ
33.	Ⓐ	Ⓑ	Ⓒ	Ⓓ	67.	Ⓐ	Ⓑ	Ⓒ	Ⓓ					
34.	Ⓐ	Ⓑ	Ⓒ	Ⓓ	68.	Ⓐ	Ⓑ	Ⓒ	Ⓓ					

Reading Comprehension

101. Ⓐ Ⓑ Ⓒ Ⓓ   135. Ⓐ Ⓑ Ⓒ Ⓓ   169. Ⓐ Ⓑ Ⓒ Ⓓ
102. Ⓐ Ⓑ Ⓒ Ⓓ   136. Ⓐ Ⓑ Ⓒ Ⓓ   170. Ⓐ Ⓑ Ⓒ Ⓓ
103. Ⓐ Ⓑ Ⓒ Ⓓ   137. Ⓐ Ⓑ Ⓒ Ⓓ   171. Ⓐ Ⓑ Ⓒ Ⓓ
104. Ⓐ Ⓑ Ⓒ Ⓓ   138. Ⓐ Ⓑ Ⓒ Ⓓ   172. Ⓐ Ⓑ Ⓒ Ⓓ
105. Ⓐ Ⓑ Ⓒ Ⓓ   139. Ⓐ Ⓑ Ⓒ Ⓓ   173. Ⓐ Ⓑ Ⓒ Ⓓ
106. Ⓐ Ⓑ Ⓒ Ⓓ   140. Ⓐ Ⓑ Ⓒ Ⓓ   174. Ⓐ Ⓑ Ⓒ Ⓓ
107. Ⓐ Ⓑ Ⓒ Ⓓ   141. Ⓐ Ⓑ Ⓒ Ⓓ   175. Ⓐ Ⓑ Ⓒ Ⓓ
108. Ⓐ Ⓑ Ⓒ Ⓓ   142. Ⓐ Ⓑ Ⓒ Ⓓ   176. Ⓐ Ⓑ Ⓒ Ⓓ
109. Ⓐ Ⓑ Ⓒ Ⓓ   143. Ⓐ Ⓑ Ⓒ Ⓓ   177. Ⓐ Ⓑ Ⓒ Ⓓ
110. Ⓐ Ⓑ Ⓒ Ⓓ   144. Ⓐ Ⓑ Ⓒ Ⓓ   178. Ⓐ Ⓑ Ⓒ Ⓓ
111. Ⓐ Ⓑ Ⓒ Ⓓ   145. Ⓐ Ⓑ Ⓒ Ⓓ   179. Ⓐ Ⓑ Ⓒ Ⓓ
112. Ⓐ Ⓑ Ⓒ Ⓓ   146. Ⓐ Ⓑ Ⓒ Ⓓ   180. Ⓐ Ⓑ Ⓒ Ⓓ
113. Ⓐ Ⓑ Ⓒ Ⓓ   147. Ⓐ Ⓑ Ⓒ Ⓓ   181. Ⓐ Ⓑ Ⓒ Ⓓ
114. Ⓐ Ⓑ Ⓒ Ⓓ   148. Ⓐ Ⓑ Ⓒ Ⓓ   182. Ⓐ Ⓑ Ⓒ Ⓓ
115. Ⓐ Ⓑ Ⓒ Ⓓ   149. Ⓐ Ⓑ Ⓒ Ⓓ   183. Ⓐ Ⓑ Ⓒ Ⓓ
116. Ⓐ Ⓑ Ⓒ Ⓓ   150. Ⓐ Ⓑ Ⓒ Ⓓ   184. Ⓐ Ⓑ Ⓒ Ⓓ
117. Ⓐ Ⓑ Ⓒ Ⓓ   151. Ⓐ Ⓑ Ⓒ Ⓓ   185. Ⓐ Ⓑ Ⓒ Ⓓ
118. Ⓐ Ⓑ Ⓒ Ⓓ   152. Ⓐ Ⓑ Ⓒ Ⓓ   186. Ⓐ Ⓑ Ⓒ Ⓓ
119. Ⓐ Ⓑ Ⓒ Ⓓ   153. Ⓐ Ⓑ Ⓒ Ⓓ   187. Ⓐ Ⓑ Ⓒ Ⓓ
120. Ⓐ Ⓑ Ⓒ Ⓓ   154. Ⓐ Ⓑ Ⓒ Ⓓ   188. Ⓐ Ⓑ Ⓒ Ⓓ
121. Ⓐ Ⓑ Ⓒ Ⓓ   155. Ⓐ Ⓑ Ⓒ Ⓓ   189. Ⓐ Ⓑ Ⓒ Ⓓ
122. Ⓐ Ⓑ Ⓒ Ⓓ   156. Ⓐ Ⓑ Ⓒ Ⓓ   190. Ⓐ Ⓑ Ⓒ Ⓓ
123. Ⓐ Ⓑ Ⓒ Ⓓ   157. Ⓐ Ⓑ Ⓒ Ⓓ   191. Ⓐ Ⓑ Ⓒ Ⓓ
124. Ⓐ Ⓑ Ⓒ Ⓓ   158. Ⓐ Ⓑ Ⓒ Ⓓ   192. Ⓐ Ⓑ Ⓒ Ⓓ
125. Ⓐ Ⓑ Ⓒ Ⓓ   159. Ⓐ Ⓑ Ⓒ Ⓓ   193. Ⓐ Ⓑ Ⓒ Ⓓ
126. Ⓐ Ⓑ Ⓒ Ⓓ   160. Ⓐ Ⓑ Ⓒ Ⓓ   194. Ⓐ Ⓑ Ⓒ Ⓓ
127. Ⓐ Ⓑ Ⓒ Ⓓ   161. Ⓐ Ⓑ Ⓒ Ⓓ   195. Ⓐ Ⓑ Ⓒ Ⓓ
128. Ⓐ Ⓑ Ⓒ Ⓓ   162. Ⓐ Ⓑ Ⓒ Ⓓ   196. Ⓐ Ⓑ Ⓒ Ⓓ
129. Ⓐ Ⓑ Ⓒ Ⓓ   163. Ⓐ Ⓑ Ⓒ Ⓓ   197. Ⓐ Ⓑ Ⓒ Ⓓ
130. Ⓐ Ⓑ Ⓒ Ⓓ   164. Ⓐ Ⓑ Ⓒ Ⓓ   198. Ⓐ Ⓑ Ⓒ Ⓓ
131. Ⓐ Ⓑ Ⓒ Ⓓ   165. Ⓐ Ⓑ Ⓒ Ⓓ   199. Ⓐ Ⓑ Ⓒ Ⓓ
132. Ⓐ Ⓑ Ⓒ Ⓓ   166. Ⓐ Ⓑ Ⓒ Ⓓ   200. Ⓐ Ⓑ Ⓒ Ⓓ
133. Ⓐ Ⓑ Ⓒ Ⓓ   167. Ⓐ Ⓑ Ⓒ Ⓓ
134. Ⓐ Ⓑ Ⓒ Ⓓ   168. Ⓐ Ⓑ Ⓒ Ⓓ